ORIGINAL
TRIUMPH
BONNEVILLE

Other titles available in the *Original* series are:

Original AC Ace & Cobra
by Rinsey Mills
Original Aston Martin DB4/5/6
by Robert Edwards
Original Austin Seven
by Rinsey Mills
Original Austin-Healey (100 & 3000)
by Anders Ditlev Clausager
Original Citroën DS
by John Reynolds with Jan de Lange
Original Corvette 1953-1962
by Tom Falconer
Original Corvette 1963-1967
by Tom Falconer
Original Ferrari V8
by Keith Bluemel
Original Ferrari V12 1965-1973
by Keith Bluemel
Original Honda CB750
by John Wyatt
Original Jaguar E-Type
by Philip Porter
Original Jaguar Mark I/II
by Nigel Thorley
Original Jaguar XJ
by Nigel Thorley
Original Jaguar XK
by Philip Porter
Original Kawasaki Z1, Z900 & KZ900
by Dave Marsden
Original Land-Rover Series I
by James Taylor
Original Mercedes SL
by Laurence Meredith
Original MG T Series
by Anders Ditlev Clausager

Original MGA
by Anders Ditlev Clausager
Original MGB
by Anders Ditlev Clausager
Original Mini Cooper and Cooper S
by John Parnell
Original Morgan
by John Worrall and Liz Turner
Original Morris Minor
by Ray Newell
Original Porsche 356
by Laurence Meredith
Original Porsche 911
by Peter Morgan
Original Porsche 924/944/968
by Peter Morgan
Original Range Rover Carburettor Models
by James Taylor
Original Rolls-Royce & Bentley 1946-65
by James Taylor
Original Sprite & Midget
by Terry Horler
Original Triumph TR2/3/3A
by Bill Piggott
Original Triumph TR4/4A/5/6
by Bill Piggott
Original Triumph TR7/8
by Bill Piggott
Original Triumph Stag
by James Taylor
Original Vincent
by J. P. Bickerstaff
Original VW Beetle
by Laurence Meredith
Original VW Bus
by Laurence Meredith

ORIGINAL
TRIUMPH
BONNEVILLE

by Gerard Kane

Photography by James Mann
Edited by Mick Duckworth

BAY
VIEW
BOOKS
FROM
MBI Publishing
Company

First published in 2000 by MBI Publishing Company, 729 Prospect Avenue, PO Box 1, Osceola, WI 54020-0001 USA

MBI Publishing Company books are also available at discounts in bulk quantity for industrial or sales-promotional use. For details write to Special Sales Manager at Motorbooks International Wholesalers & Distributors, 729 Prospect Avenue, PO Box 1, Osceola, WI 54020-0001 USA.

Library of Congress Cataloging-in-Publication Data Available

ISBN 0-7603-0776-8

The photographs on the jacket and preliminary pages show examples of 1964 US-market T120R (front cover), 1965 US-market T120C TT Special (frontispiece), 1962 UK-market T120 (title page), 1982 UK-market T140LE Royal (contents page) and 1959 UK-market T120 (back cover).

Series edited by Mark Hughes
Designed by Chris Fayers

Printed in China

Contents

Introduction

A certain style and panache has always made Triumph twins stand out from other classic British motorcycles. Lithe and functional-looking, these products of the Meriden factory have a pleasing symmetry about them, and are often finished in imaginative and tasteful colours.

In post-war Britain, struggling out of the grip of austerity, Triumph brought glamour to motorcycling more than any other marque. Other makes had their admirers, of course, but if you were to have asked non-motorcyclists to name a make of two-wheeler, the chances are they would have said 'Triumph'. And by the 1960s, one particular model personified the Triumph name – the potent Bonneville. Not just a stunning looker, this 650cc twin had a reputation for scorching acceleration and a top speed in excess of 110mph that few others could match.

Even today the Bonneville name, derived from America's most famous speed records venue, is widely recalled by enthusiast and non-enthusiast alike. The machine has become an icon of its age. Indeed, the name is still so evocative that it has been held in reserve by John Bloor, owner of the Triumph identity since 1983. Bloor has made a deserved success of reviving Triumph as a modern motorcycle manufacturer and has adopted most of the old model names to help market his new machines. The Bonnevilles of the 21st Century are likely to be fine machines judging by the record so far of Bloor's current plant at Hinckley.

But for many, the definitive 'Bonnie' will always be a sporting air-cooled parallel twin, born in the 1950s and surviving in updated form through to the 1980s. This book deals in depth with this design – the original Bonneville.

Such is the enduring popularity of the T120 and later 750cc T140 that even today a keen and knowledgeable restorer could probably build up a complete machine from new parts. That is a measure of the Bonneville's success. The drawback of this success to the prospective restorer is that relatively few Bonnevilles have remained exactly as they were the day they left the factory. Inevitably braking and electrical systems have often been improved to help cope with modern traffic conditions. Thousands of T120s were mod-ified in the late 1960s' craze for customising and creating café racers. And in latter years some ill-informed restorers have finished machines with non-standard parts, incorrect details or unoriginal colour finishes.

This book aims to outline the original specifications and trim for each year, showing what the particular models would have looked like when new and helping present-day enthusiasts in their quest for authenticity.

Many restorers seem to concentrate on cosmetics, but while this provides a favourable first impression, it is surely just as important to devote the same degree of attention to the unseen mechanical parts. After all, the finished product should be a functioning motorcycle, not merely an ornament. For this reason, I aim to cover engine specification changes as well as other less obvious variations throughout the Bonneville's long production run in as much detail as the outward appearance of the machine.

For many the ultimate pleasure of a classic machine will always be the riding. If being out on the road is your primary concern, a Bonneville will certainly not disappoint. It can make an eminently practical machine, especially if a little judicious modernisation and improvement is carried out by the owner. Whether meticulously restoring a Bonneville to dead-original or preparing a machine to ride and enjoy every day, the important thing is to remember why you are doing it. If it gives you pleasure, you are on the right track.

Acknowledgments

In the course of preparing this book, a number of people have been extremely generous, not only with their time and expertise, but in allowing their cherished machinery to be photographed by James Mann. I am indebted to Graham Bowen, Bill Crosby of Reg Allen Motorcycles and the London Motorcycle Museum, Clive Humphries, Dennis Middleton, Cliff Rushworth of Ace Classics, and Tony Sumner. For furnishing superb machines in the USA, I thank Robert Sullivan of Hanson, Massachusetts, and Performance Cycles of Shrewsbury, Massachusetts. Thanks also to former Triumph manager John Nelson and Roy Shilling of the Triumph Owners MCC for their help with illustrations. For their assistance in checking information, Hughie Hancox and John Healy have my heartfelt gratitude. Both are mines of information and have been unstinting in their assistance.

The legendary Bonneville in its earliest form. Tangerine and Pearl Grey was a bold colour choice in 1959.

Chapter 1

Background to the Bonneville's Birth

The Bonneville did not happen overnight. Nor was it a completely new, ground-breaking model, wildly different from anything Triumph had produced before. It was a slow distillation of what was best in the existing range. Although it was wholly designed and manufactured in Britain, the input from Triumph's American agents cannot be over-emphasised. It is not merely in name that the Bonneville owes a debt to the USA.

Because of the Bonneville's lengthy gestation period and its long ancestral line, it is worth taking a brief look at its antecedents and the history of the firm that gave the world such an enduring motorcycling legend.

Early years

Perhaps surprisingly for a marque that has become so quintessentially British, Triumph was actually founded by two Germans. As long ago as 1888, Siegfried Bettmann, who had been a bicycle dealer in London, and engineer Mauritz Shulte set up a factory in Coventry to manufacture bicycles. The Triumph name was chosen for no better reason than because it carried the right connotations for the successful business that Bettmann and Shulte hoped it would become.

It was not long before the partners decided to jump on the motor-bicycle bandwagon. At first, they used a proprietary engine clipped to a suitably modified frame from one of their own cycles, but in 1905 their own power unit appeared, designed by Shulte and Charles Hathaway.

World War I significantly furthered the reputation of the company and its products, which by then were proper motorcycles. The 500cc Model H side-valve single, introduced in 1914, became the despatch rider's trusted friend and nearly 30,000 of these rugged machines saw service with Allied forces.

After the war, there was a boom in motorcycle sales as the young men who had ridden them in the services returned home reluctant to do without their Trusty Triumphs. By 1920, annual output from the Coventry plant was running at 10,000 machines, and nine years later it was up to an incredible 30,000 units. During the intervening years, new models arrived to supplement the Model H. The overhead, four-valve Model R, designed by Henry Ricardo, appeared in 1922, followed by the 500cc Model TT, the 350cc Model LS and the budget Model P.

Entering the 1930s, Triumph faced the same problems as many other manufacturers. When the Depression was about to hit Britain, Triumph continued to chase customers by expanding its range still further. Designer Val Page was recruited from the Ariel factory in 1932, and set about updating the entire Triumph catalogue. Topping the new range was the firm's first vertical twin: giving little hint of the successes to come for that engine layout, the overweight, hand-change twin – best suited to sidecar pulling – was not a big seller.

Since 1923, the company had also been producing cars and had ploughed money into ensuring racing successes for its works team at Le Mans. More and more resources were being directed towards car manufacture. With such profligate spending on all fronts, something had to give. The bicycle sector of the company was sold off to Raleigh in 1932, and there was mounting pressure on the board to concentrate solely on car production. Founding father Siegfried Bettmann retired in 1933 and the mood for major change grew stronger. It finally came early in 1936, when Ariel boss Jack Sangster became the new owner of Triumph's motorcycle operations.

The Speed Twin

The new enterprise was to trade under the name of The Triumph Engineering Company. Sangster's first move was to engage Ariel's chief designer, Edward Turner, as managing director. Turner's inspired designs had revived Ariel's fortunes and Sangster hoped his protégé could repeat the formula with the ailing Triumph concern. It was to prove an inspired decision. Straight away, Turner re-packaged the Page-designed singles and axed the 650cc twin. The Tiger range of sporting singles was born and proved an overnight success. But the design that was to make the whole motorcycling world sit up and take notice was just around the corner. Towards the end of 1937,

The event that initiated the Bonneville legend. Johnny Allen streaks across the Bonneville Salt Flats course in the Texas-built 650cc Triumph streamliner to set a new world record at 214.17mph in September 1956, as depicted in a painting by J.E. Davies. *Courtesy of John Nelson*

650 c.c. Unsupercharged TRIUMPH breaks World Motorcycle Speed Record at 214 m.p.h. Bonneville Salt Flats, Utah, 6th Sept. 1956. Rider JOHNNY ALLEN

Turner unveiled his 5T Speed Twin.

Here, at last, was a twin-cylinder motorcycle for the masses. Costing just £5 more (and weighing 5lbs less) than the single-cylinder Tiger 90, Turner's 500cc parallel twin changed the face of the British motorcycle industry. The Speed Twin proved that a compact multi-cylinder machine could be a volume seller. Housed in the same frame and utilising the same gearbox as the Tiger 90, the twin-cylinder engine was barely any wider than a single. This was made possible by the design of the crankshaft, which was bolted together in three parts with the flywheel at its centre. The motor's 360-degree crank pin configuration was destined to become a hallmark of the British industry for decades.

A one-piece cast-iron barrel was fixed to the alloy crankcases by six studs and nuts. At the top, the iron cylinder head employed eight bolts to attach it to the barrels. Camshafts were gear-driven from the crankshaft and mounted front and rear, operating the valve gear via pushrods inside chromed tubes tucked into the cylinder fins. Inlet and exhaust rocker spindles housed in separate rocker boxes carried two rockers each, with screw-on caps for clearance adjustment. A single carburettor fed parallel inlet tracts, while outwardly splayed exhaust ports mimicked the look of 1930s' twin-port singles.

But if the new machine looked like a single, it certainly did not perform or sound like one. Riders were immediately impressed by the lively acceleration of the twin. And after years of familiarity with the flat bark of singles, the hard-edged rasp of the new Triumph when revved hard was music to enthusiasts' ears. A mere two years on from the Sangster take-over, Triumph was struggling to meet the demands of eager customers rather than creditors. Whatever they were paying Turner, it probably was not enough!

A sports version of the Speed Twin followed in 1939. Called the Tiger 100, to follow the sequence established by the single-cylinder machines, the new model made 8bhp more than the 5T and as the name implied, its claimed top speed was a magic 'ton'. The extra power came from a raised compression ratio, larger carburettor and polished engine internals. Demand for the sporty Tiger outstripped that for the already very popular Speed Twin, but escalating sales were halted by the outbreak of World War II.

Like the rest of industry, Triumph pitched in to the war effort with vigour, being kept busy on production of military motorcycles, generator sets and other equipment. On the night of 14 November 1940, when the centre of Coventry was all but wiped out in a massive air raid, Triumph's factory received a number of direct hits and was virtually destroyed. With the spirit that typified war-time Britain, everything that could be salvaged was installed in a nearby building and production resumed within weeks. Government help was

promised in locating a new factory, and within only 18 months Triumph moved to a new plant outside Coventry on Meriden Road, Allesley, near the village of Meriden. Every cloud has a silver lining: when the war ended in 1945, Triumph was poised to resume commercial production with a modern factory and a range of highly attractive twin-cylinder machines.

But raw materials were in short supply and the cost of the war to the UK economy was becoming apparent. For Triumph, like other manufacturers, exports were the priority. The Meriden factory's approach to post-war reconstruction was to rationalise its model range. Out went the pre-war Tiger singles, leaving the best-selling twins to occupy the production lines.

Edward Turner was not only a gifted designer, but also a shrewd businessman. During the immediate post-war era, when money and resources were scarce, he resisted change as far as possible. The Triumph range consisted of only the Speed Twin and T100 until 1947, when the 500cc twins were joined by the 350cc 3T. Apart from the introduction of Turner's sprung-hub rear suspension system, available as an option from 1947, the range continued largely unchanged until late

1948, when the Grand Prix racing model and the on/off-road Trophy TR5 arrived. These specialised 500s had all-alloy engines with 'square barrel' top ends derived from the type used in Triumph's war-time fan-cooled stationary generators supplied for airborne use.

Bigger engines for America

A really important model was launched for the 1950 season. The 6T Thunderbird was Turner's first over-500cc twin and the reason for its appearance was largely attributable to Triumph's North American importers. In the post-war climate the US export market was the key to commercial growth, and Triumph's advantage was that Turner knew the territory well.

Since pre-war times, Triumph sales in Western USA had been handled by Johnson Motors Inc of Pasadena, California, run by Turner's enthusiastic friend Bill Johnson, businessman Wilbur Ceder and racer-tuner Pete Colman. And by 1950, the Meriden-owned Triumph Corporation was being set up in Baltimore, Maryland, to serve the Eastern, South-Eastern and Mid-Western states, run by English-born Denis McCormack.

Superb 1950 Thunderbird, restored by Triumph specialist Hughie Hancox, hints at things to come. The Bonneville's heritage can be traced back even earlier, to the 500cc Speed Twin.

An outstanding example of the T120 Bonneville as it first appeared, to a stunning welcome, at the 1958 Earls Court Show.

There was fierce and – for Triumph – healthy competition between the eastern and western operations but on one subject they were in complete agreement. To achieve more success in a market where typical US-built heavyweights were of 45 cubic inches (750cc), a larger motor would be required. Hence the 650cc Thunderbird.

At a casual glance, its 649cc motor looked identical to the Speed Twin and Tiger 100 units, but increasing the bore from 63mm to 71mm and the stroke from 80mm to 82mm made an appreciable difference. With its improved power-to-weight ratio, the 6T Thunderbird would hit 100mph with relative ease and its mid-range torque made touring riding at respectable speeds a doddle. So confident was Edward Turner in his new model that he despatched three bikes and five riders plus a support crew to the banked racing circuit at Montlhéry, near Paris. The trio of Thunderbirds were ridden to the track and hammered round the banking at an average speed in excess of 90mph for 500 miles before being ridden back to the factory. It was a masterful piece of promotion for Triumph's new top-of-the-range machine.

Receiving a warm welcome in Britain, the 6T was to become a red-hot seller in the 'States.

Competition success was important to sales there and private tuners were not slow to capitalise on the T-bird's extra cubic inches. They found the tried-and-tested route that proved successful on 500cc motors – raising compression ratios, re-profiling cams, gas-flowing cylinder heads – paid similar performance dividends on the 650s. It came as no surprise, therefore, when the factory announced the sports version of the Thunderbird, the Tiger 110, in late 1953.

The T110 ('Ton-ten') code clearly hinted at the new 650's speed potential. The latest Tiger incorporated the proven modifications of the US tuners, but the uprated engine also benefited from being housed in Triumph's first frame with swinging arm suspension. A larger carburettor, higher-lift E3325 camshafts, bigger valves and higher-compression pistons gave the T110 its extra go, while at the front, a larger 8in brake helped in hauling up the lively twin. The press were ecstatic over the new model, recording 117mph on an ostensibly standard machine in full road trim.

While the Thunderbird and Tiger 110 hogged the limelight during the early 1950s, Triumph was not ignoring the 500cc category. The rigid-frame TR5, called the Trophy to celebrate works team success in the 1948 International Six Days Trial, was intended as a genuine dual-purpose on/off-road competition machine. Since overhead valve engines were limited to 500cc for many US racing events, Triumph also marketed a tuning kit for the Tiger 100, which now had a handsome all-alloy engine with close-pitched cylinder fins.

Triumph was taken over by the BSA organisation in 1952, but the Meriden plant remained largely autonomous and prospered at home and abroad in the late 1950s. The Tiger 110 was the king of the road and, at the other end of the scale, the little 200cc ohv single-cylinder Tiger Cub made inroads into the novice and commuter markets. Who could ask for more?

The Americans, of course! In September 1956, Texan Johnny Allen powered a Thunderbird-engined streamliner to a new absolute motorcycle speed record of 214mph at the Bonneville Salt Flats course near Wendover, Utah. The achievement was to inspire the birth of a legend.

The engine of Allen's machine had been built by Texan tuner Jack Wilson, based at a Triumph dealership run by Pete Dalio in Fort Worth. It was installed in a body shell created by the initiator of the project, Texan aviator JH 'Stormy' Mangham. Fuelled by methanol with 65 per cent nitro-methane, and equipped with a one-piece 'billet' crankshaft, Cadillac car big ends and a pair of 1⅜in Amal GP track carburettors, the projectile's unsupercharged power unit was still essentially an iron-headed 6T motor.

Although there were to be protracted political wrangles over the record's official status outside the USA, the 214mph run was a stunning publicity coup for Meriden. As news of the success spread, so did demand for yet more performance from the standard models, particularly in the 'States. Triumph would not to be rushed though, and demands for higher speeds were usually met by referring to competition tuning parts already catalogued by the factory. Although Edward Turner was overjoyed by Allen's achievement, he had always opposed spending too much time or money on racing and competition projects.

For 1956, the T110 and a new 650cc TR6 Trophy model were fitted with an alloy cylinder head to deal better with increased temperatures generated by higher compression ratios, made possible by the availability of higher octane fuels. Known in factory parlance as the Delta Head, the new casting also dispensed with external rocker box drain pipes, now routing oil down through the pushrod tubes. For the following year, Meriden built a batch of 500cc Tiger 100/RS racers for the USA with a twin-carburettor Delta head, listed separately as a tuning aid in a Tri-Cor catalogue and stimulating demand for a version to fit the 650 engine. Eventually, in 1958 a twin-carburettor head for 650s with splayed inlet ports appeared in a replacement parts list.

The Bonneville arrives

It was not until late 1958, when 1959 models were already rolling off the production line, that Triumph's management agreed to give the public what it clearly wanted.

Earlier that year, an experimental machine had been tested at the Motor Industry Research Association (MIRA) proving grounds near Nuneaton, Warwickshire. The motor installed in the prototype, a T110 unit with a twin inlet port head, E3134 racing cams and 8.5:1 compression ratio, had produced 48.8bhp on the factory dynamometer. And making the whole project feasible was a sturdy new one-piece crankshaft developed for the 1959 models.

Triumph's original bolted-up three-piece shaft had been used largely unchanged, except for the introduction of a bigger timing-side main bearing journal on 500s and 650s for 1954; ever-rising output had created problems in maintaining shaft alignment under full power. The new forged crank, with its pressed and bolted-on central ring flywheel, allowed full rein to be given to the twin-carb motor. The bottom end was not the only area which had come under pressure from increased output: the six-plate T110 clutch was nearing its limits, while the single-leading-shoe front brake gave factory tester Percy Tait a few heart-stopping moments at MIRA.

As head of the experimental department, ace tuner Frank Baker was in charge of preparing the prototype. After the successful MIRA test, similar machines were assembled and shaken down on both road and track by the factory's team of testers. The results were encouraging and, at a meeting in August 1958, Edward Turner gave the 'twin-carb T110' project the green light. Although the 1959 sales literature had already been prepared and the Earls Court Show was imminent, the new model was to be included in the 1959 line-up. Misprinted as a 500cc machine in the hastily revised price list (the mistake was covered up by over-printing 'ohv twin 650cc'), Triumph's new range-topper did not even make it into the '59 catalogue. However, it did appear at the show, where it instantly became the star attraction. In recognition of Allen's 1956 record-breaking exploits, the new model was called the T120 Bonneville.

That sensational Earls Court launch was the start of a long story. Over the next 30 years the Bonneville would be improved, revised, updated and enlarged. A vast selection of aftermarket tuning and styling parts would become available and competition variants of the T120 would earn their place in history.

Chapter 2

Launch of the Legend: 1959

Whatever the rushed circumstances of its last-minute inclusion in the 1959 model line-up, the Bonneville certainly created a stir. Although it may have appeared to the casual observer to have been little more than a twin-carburettor T110, the reality for enthusiasts was that the T120's whole was more than the sum of its parts. Production of Meriden's new flagship actually began on 4 September 1958 with engine unit 020377.

The T120 made a bold visual statement, the striking Pearl Grey and Tangerine finish of its petrol tank and mudguards setting the new sports

Start of a long line: a 1959 UK Bonneville restored to original condition.

Trademark of the Bonneville (facing page): the splayed-inlet twin-carburettor cylinder head.

Valve clearance data transfer is accurately located on engine plates' shroud. Cork gasket seals joint where dynamo fastens to timing chest.

Oil filler plug on primary drive cover is embossed with lubricant guide: today's owners tend to use automatic transmission fluid.

US-market T120 for 1959 is identifiable by smaller fuel tank and raised handlebars preferred by American riders – but tank-top parcel rack and headlamp nacelle were not popular in the 'States.

twin apart at a time when most British machines had more sombre colour schemes. The first Bonneville took its styling cues from the Tiger 110, even retaining the nacelle headlamp enclosure which was to prove unpopular in the USA. The colour choice was also less than universally welcomed and, later in the model year, the option of a more restrained scheme of Pearl Grey (actually a pale blue) and Azure Blue was made available. All in all, though, the Bonneville was a success from the start. The factory had got it mostly right with the 404lb, 46bhp twin: Triumph had given speed enthusiasts what they had been asking for.

Engine

Based as it was on the Tiger 110 engine, the Bonneville's motor shared much with that unit. The 360-degree, 649cc vertical twin engine featured a conventional overhead valve layout with two camshafts (E3134 profile inlet, E3325 exhaust) driven via an idler gear from a pinion on the right-hand end of the crankshaft.

At the drive-side end of the inlet cam, a rotary timed breather relieved excess crankcase pressure. The camshafts, running in bush bearings in the crankcase and sited one ahead of the cylinder block and one behind, operated followers situated in blocks pressed into the base of the barrel casting. From these, alloy pushrods – encased in separate chromed steel tubes recessed in the cylinder finning at front and rear – actuated the rockers. Housed in detachable alloy rocker boxes, the rockers themselves ran on two separate spindles, one each for exhaust and inlet. They operated valves with diameters of 1⅛in (inlet) and 1½in (exhaust), controlled by dual coil springs. Four separate, circular inspection covers threaded into the rocker box covers gave access for valve clearance adjustment. Drains inside the rocker boxes routed oil down the pushrod tubes, which were sealed at top and bottom by square-section neoprene O-rings.

The cylinder block was a one-piece iron casting, with a small air gap between the bores to aid cooling. At its base flange, it fixed to eight studs threaded into the crankcase. On top of the barrels, the die-cast alloy cylinder head, with its trademark splayed inlet tracts, was held to the block by eight ⅜in bolts.

This cylinder head was not a totally new casting, being an adapted version of the parallel-port Tiger 110 head; unmachined remnants of the original tracts and the earlier casting number (E3548) were visible below the intake rocker box. Flanged carburettor mounting stubs were screwed into the threaded inlets and secured by large nuts on the external threaded portion of the stubs.

At the front of the cylinder head, the exhaust

pipes fitted over cast stubs retained by finned clamps. As on the T110, 1½in pipes and straight-through 'cigar' silencers with a slight upward tilt at the rear were fitted. With noise legislation looming, the silencers were replaced from engine number 024337 by internally baffled versions which retained the same external shape.

The rest of the engine was much the same as the T110. Cast alloy pistons giving a compression ratio of 8.5:1 were of thicker section at the crown than the previous year's components, but, even so, some gave trouble. Piston crown thickness was increased twice more in the first year of production. Piston skirts also came in for modification after several failures were reported after sustained hard use. This time, the problem was resolved by machining the skirts to give greater clearance

Float bowl cover screws on Monobloc carburettors are lockwired to resist vibration. Short chromed bell-mouths are correct, but wire should really be twisted.

between them and the crankshaft bobweights. For those seeking even higher performance, pistons of 12:1 compression ratio plus racing valve springs and guides were catalogued.

The Bonneville shared a revised one-piece, forged EN16B crankshaft with the rest of the 1959 650 twins. A cast-iron flywheel was bolted radially to the centre of the shaft after being passed over the timing-side outer web. Initially there were problems with flywheel bolt breakage, but increasing the tightness of the initial interference fit of the flywheel over the crankshaft centre web solved this. After engine number 027610 new flywheel bolts were fitted as an added precaution. The crankshaft was supported by two ballrace main bearings located in the crankcase halves.

H-section connecting rods in RR56 alloy featured detachable shell bearings in their big ends. A pair of high-tensile stretch bolts secured each big-end cap, while the small-end bearings were plain bushes.

A double-plunger pump, driven by an eccentric peg on the nut securing the inlet camshaft pinion, took care of the dry sump engine's lubrication. The big ends were fed via by drillings in the crank, end-fed at pressure from oilways in the timing cover, the latter supporting both the nose of the crank and the camshaft drive idler pinion in plain bushes. Externally, the cover bore the distinctive triangular Triumph patent plate, held by rivets. Incidentally, early Bonnevilles wore 'Tiger 110' patent plates, but later models carried the '650 Twin' plate as worn by the Thunderbird.

A pressure-relief valve in the lower timing cover protected the system and a tell-tale pressure indicator was provided on its domed housing. On the underside of the crankcase, a removable sump plate was bolted to a rectangular protrusion. When oil drained into the sump, it passed through a mesh strainer screen held between the plate and the crankcase. It was then scavenged back to the oil tank and, via a T-piece in the return line, also routed externally up to the rocker spindles.

Even though the first year of Bonneville production did not pass without a few engine problems, overall it was a successful launch.

Remote float chamber is between carburettors. Mounting to frame can be seen at rear.

MINIMUM OIL LEVEL

Fuel system & carburettors

Onto the Bonneville's instantly recognisable splayed inlet tracts were mounted two 1¹⁄₁₆in Amal Monobloc carburettors with their float bowls removed. These 'chopped' Monoblocs were a tight fit under the petrol tank and fuel taps, so it is important when restoring a 1959 model to use the correct carburettor tops if the various components are not to foul one another. Neither carburettor had a tickler button, but one was provided on the remote float chamber. Each had a short chromed bellmouth at the intake.

On early machines, jets and settings were the same for both UK/general export and US models. Main jet size was 240, pilot jet 25 and needle jet 0.1065. A 376 slide was fitted with a 3½ cutaway and the needle was a type C in position 3.

Giving some indication of the factory's concern with the vibration inevitably generated by a 360-degree twin, the covers for the apertures where the float bowls had been removed were lockwired in place. All three fixing screws' heads were drilled and the lockwire formed a closed triangle on each cover. An Amal 14/617 float bowl, as used with the GP track carburettor, was rubber-mounted from a block attached centrally on the

frame's main vertical tube. It was top-fed via a two-way banjo union from twin taps on either side of the petrol tank, and a T-piece in the fuel line from the remote bowl to the carburettors distributed petrol evenly. The valances of both the unused air filter box and the oil tank had to be modified to clear the float bowl.

This makeshift arrangement proved troublesome, since the float bowl was prone to fuel surge under hard acceleration or braking. In an effort to combat this, a modification was introduced late in the season, moving the bowl further forward to a position between the carburettor bodies. By this time, though, many owners had discovered that the simplest cure for the problem was to fit two conventional Monoblocs.

Transmission

Like the rest of the machine, the pre-unit Bonneville's four-speed gearbox was not fresh from the Meriden drawing boards. Rather it was the most recent evolution of a 'box used on Edward Turner's seminal Speed Twin. Of course there had been changes, but it was of the same layout, with a mainshaft and layshaft, arranged one above the other. Situated behind the engine, the gearbox

Some very early 1959 Bonnevilles wore T110 patent plates. This machine from later in the year has a simpler plate listing patent numbers only.

was housed in its own separate alloy housing which was cast in three sections. Fairly conventional at the time, it followed the traditional British pattern, having drive input and output on the same side – at the left-side end of the mainshaft. The same case-hardened mainshaft and layshaft pinions as on the T110 were used.

A positive-stop foot-change mechanism operated by the rider's right foot moved a quadrant which, in turn, engaged with a vertically-mounted camplate pivoted in a bush held in the gearbox casing. A track in the camplate engaged with rollers on two gear selector forks – running on a common spindle – to slide the pinions along their shafts. Under the camplate, at the bottom of the gearbox main casing, was a spring-loaded plunger, which engaged in indentations on the outside edge of the camplate to provide correct indexing of the gears. Early camplates suffered in US competition use, particularly desert racing, so from engine number 023941 the periphery of the camplate was induction hardened.

The gearbox mainshaft was supported by ball journal bearings at both ends. On the drive side, the mainshaft passed through the top gear pinion, which actually ran in the ballrace and provided the mounting for the gearbox output sprocket, which, in turn, was secured by a large nut outside the casing. On the other side of the gearbox, the mainshaft was supported by a bearing in the inner of the two end covers. The clutch pushrod ran through the centre of the mainshaft, being operated by a lever pivoting in the outer cover.

The layshaft made do with two bushes, pegged into the gearbox main casing at one end and the inner cover at the other, where a ten-tooth pinion for the speedometer drive was fitted by means of a peg through a drilling in the shaft. An eight-tooth pinion was also available to suit the optional wide-ratio gear cluster if fitted. Towards the rear of the gearbox outer cover and just astern of the gear-change was the kick-start lever, secured to its shaft by a cotter pin. The shaft pivoted in a bush in the case, and on its inner end, behind a coiled-leaf return spring, was a toothed quadrant engaging with a spring-loaded pinion on the mainshaft. From there, kick-starter movement was transmitted through a ratchet splined to the end of the shaft and secured by a lock washer. An oil drain plug was provided in the main casing and a level plug at the bottom of the inner gearbox cover.

The Slickshift mechanism, designed to aid brisk gear-changing by transferring the movement of the gear lever to the clutch pushrod, had been standard on the T110. But on the Bonneville gearbox its operating pin and roller were absent. Riders had never taken to the Slickshift, preferring the normal manual release of the clutch.

Otherwise the transmission was pure Tiger 110, the Bonnie sharing the Tiger's 18-tooth gearbox, 46-tooth rear wheel sprockets, and 101-link ⅜in x ⅜in final drive chain. The 24-tooth engine mainshaft sprocket and 43-tooth clutch sprocket were again identical, though both wide- and close-ratio internal clusters were also available for competition use.

A two-piece alloy primary chaincase, containing ¼pt of SAE 20 oil, incorporated both filler and level plugs, and was polished on its visible surfaces. From engine number 022861, longer screws were used to fasten the outer cover to the inner. Tension of the 70-link ½in x ⁵⁄₁₆in single-row Renold primary chain was maintained by pivoting the gearbox on the lower of its two mounts, using an adjuster provided at the upper mount.

Even before the birth of the Bonneville, the 650's clutch was hard-pressed to cope with ever-increasing power output. To beef it up, a different grade of Neolangite friction material was specified for the five driven plates; the six driving plates were of plain steel. Along with above-mentioned wear at the gearbox camplate under competition conditions, the clutch sprocket centre was also found to suffer under similar use. From engine number 024029, this too received improved hardening treatment.

Four adjustable coil springs in the clutch provided pressure to transmit drive, and the clutch drum and sprocket ran on 20 hardened steel rollers between it and the clutch hub. The clutch centre incorporated a transmission shock absorber in the form of a vaned 'spider' keyed to the mainshaft with rubber inserts between it and the clutch centre to cushion the drive.

Frame & rear suspension

Since 1955, Triumph's 650s had swinging arm rear suspension, first seen on the 1954 Tiger 110. The Bonneville's frame was identical to that of the 1959 T110, the benefit to restorers being that parts from either machine of that year are correct.

The frame followed traditional industry practice, being a single downtube cradle type made in two sections, front and rear. Tubes were joined by being brazed into cast lugs, and the two separate parts of the frame bolted together at the top of the seat post and below the swinging arm pivot lugs. Overall, the dimensions of the frame and swinging arm gave the Bonneville a wheelbase of 55¼in and a head angle of 64½ degrees. Triumph's new Easy-lift centre stand was fitted as standard and there was provision for both the prop stand and a steering lock. The rider's footrests mounted on the engine plates between the engine and gearbox. An extended through-bolt, threaded at its extremities, passed through the plates and the primary chaincase, and the footrests' inner bosses fitted over its outer extremities to be secured by nuts on the threads. To prevent the footrests rotating, their bosses had two pegs on the inner faces which engaged in corresponding holes in the primary chaincase and right-side engine plate.

The silencers and pivoting pillion footrests shared brackets, which were bolted to the frame on each side behind the swinging arm pivot. These were enamelled black to match the frame, as were the engine plates, which were fixed to both crankcase and frame by through-bolts with spring washers under their nuts to prevent loosening through vibration.

Supplied by Girling, the rear suspension units were hydraulically-damped with a spring rate of 100lb/in. Although adjustable for pre-load, these sealed units had no means of varying the damping. Their sheet steel upper shrouds were finished in black, while the lower covers were chromed.

Alternative spring rates could be specified by the purchaser, with both 150lb/in sidecar, plus 130 and 110lb/in solo units being available, as well as 90lb/in racing springs. Metal Oilite bushes were used to pivot the swinging arm, which was of tubular construction and also finished in black. The long rear brake pedal, traditionally mounted on the rider's left, operated the rear drum via a rod with a threaded hand-adjuster at the rear.

Although it had proved just about adequate for the lower-powered Thunderbird and Tiger 110, the frame was not the 1959 Bonneville's finest feature. Handling could get distinctly interesting if the engine's 46bhp was used as intended. The fact that the T120 was to be completely revised for 1960 lends weight to the theory that the 1959 launch of the Bonneville was rushed.

Steering & front suspension

The conventional telescopic fork had internal coil springs and a one-way damper assembly controlling rebound only. Springs were available in differing grades, colour-coded by blobs of paint: red denoted the standard solo spring, with blue for sidecar use and purple for extra-heavy sidecar use. Why anyone would have wanted 1959's hottest sports twin for extra-heavy sidecar use is puzzling, but the option was there anyway!

A friction steering damper was adjusted by a large black-enamelled cast knob on the top yoke. This operated through the steering stem by tightening or loosening a pair of friction discs on the underside of the lower yoke.

Cup-and-cone ball bearings were employed in the steering head, while the 1in-diameter handlebars were clamped into semi-circular recesses in the top yoke casting by means of steel U-bolts which passed through the cast-iron top yoke, to be secured from underneath by four ⁵⁄₁₆in nuts with

Rear wheel details, showing brake rod arrangement, deep chainguard and embossed pillion footrest rubbers.

Original bolt with maker's name visible on head; this one locates the top of the rear suspension unit. The Triumph factory used fasteners from various suppliers.

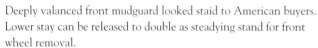
Deeply valanced front mudguard looked staid to American buyers. Lower stay can be released to double as steadying stand for front wheel removal.

Right side of front wheel shows single-leading-shoe brake drum, alloy backplate and operating lever. Wheel is 19in, with 40 spokes and chromed rim.

spring washers. Bonnevilles for the home or general export (non-US) markets received fairly low, slightly swept-back 'bars. Machines for the 'States wore the more flamboyant high-rise 'bars favoured by US riders, although these looked slightly ill-at-ease with the headlamp nacelle. In mid-season, handlebars on UK and general export models changed to a straighter, sportier shape. Optional dropped 'bars for road racing were also available, with a special bend to suit the nacelle; these were of smaller (⅞in) diameter, necessitating adaptor shims in the clamps and a different set of control fittings and hand grips.

Although early publicity photographs and the parts book for 1959 show home-market Bonnevilles having pressed steel brake and clutch control levers without ball ends, photos of the US-model production line in 1959 show ball-

ended levers in place. It seems likely that few, if any, 1959 Bonnevilles arrived at dealers with the pressed-steel type.

By using a one-into-two splitter box in the throttle cable, the standard T110 twistgrip with its spring-loaded friction adjuster could be used to control throttle slides in two carburettors.

Both handlebar grips were of black rubber with the Triumph name moulded into them. On the left side, the combined horn and dip-switch – fixed by a saddle clamp to the clutch lever pivot – was joined by an ignition advance/retard lever mounted further inboard.

The headlamp nacelle was not much admired, particularly in the USA. Already present on the T110, 6T and T100, the two-part pressed steel cowling sat uneasily with the Bonneville's image. Finished in black with a chromed horn grille

below the inset headlamp at the front, the upper and lower halves were clamped together by the headlamp rim, plus chromed strips on each side. Two small screws at the rear attached it to the fork covers. Rubber grommets protected cables and wires from chafing with handlebar movement where they passed into the nacelle.

Wheels, brakes & tyres

Also shared with the T110, the finned, black-enamelled, 8in-diameter, full-width front hub, with its integral brake drum, ran on a pair of ball races. The left-side bearing was retained by a circlip outside its dust cover, while the right-side bearing was held in place by a threaded retaining ring which screwed into the centre of the hub. It is important to note when dismantling this type of hub that this ring has a left-hand thread. The right-side bearing also had a backing ring against which a shoulder on the wheel spindle butted up. Forty identical, 8/10G x 5⅜in, cadmium-plated,

straight-pull spokes laced the hub to a chromium-plated 19in WM2-19 rim fitted with a 3.25 x 19in ribbed Dunlop tyre.

Stopping power at the front was provided by a single-leading-shoe brake assembly mounted on a polished alloy backplate, which had a slot cast integrally on its outer face that located over an anchoring tab on the right-hand fork leg. Linings were riveted to the shoes, which had return springs at either end close to the fulcrum and operating cam. A square outer end on the operating camshaft accepted the operating lever, which had its own return spring, anchored in a small drilling in the backplate. When well set-up, this brake was fairly effective, but it needed to be applied in good time if a Bonnie's full performance was unleashed!

A circular chromed cover was fitted on the left side of the hub. This cover was elaborately fluted on early models, but later reverted to a plainer type also seen on the T110.

At the rear wheel, two options were available. The standard set-up was a 7in cast-iron brake

Drive-side shots show models in US (above) and UK (opposite) forms. Elaborate front hub trim made way for a plainer version later in the year. Friction-type steering damper is visible under steering head.

drum with the 46-tooth final drive sprocket incorporated on its outer edge. This was bolted to the hub by eight nuts and bolts secured in pairs by tab washers. As at the front, the wheel ran on two ballraces and the brake was a single-leading-shoe drum with a steel backplate. At each end of the wheel spindle there was an adjuster for setting drive chain tension and wheel alignment.

As an option, Triumph also offered a Quickly Detachable (QD) rear wheel assembly on the Bonneville. Obviously this made changing the rear tyre much easier and was a justly popular fitting. The QD hub ran on three bearings rather than two. Two adjustable Timken taper-roller bearings resided in the hub itself, while there was a ballrace bearing in the brake drum's centre. The hub was splined into the brake drum and the wheel could be removed without disturbing the chain or brake assembly. All that was required was to undo the spindle nut and withdraw the spindle and its spacer from the right-hand side. The wheel could then be parted from the drum and withdrawn from the frame. Other than this feature, and the hub-to-brake drum bolts, the QD wheel was similar to the standard set-up. On both QD and bolt-up hubs, two different lengths of spokes were used, both with 90-degree heads. Left-side spokes were 8/10G x 8in and those on the right were 8/10G x 8⅜in. As on the front wheel, a WM2-19 chromed steel rim was used, this time shod with a 3.50 x 19in Dunlop Universal tyre.

Seat & bodywork

Two types of seat were specified for the 1959 Bonneville, but it is uncertain when the change was made. The first examples left the factory wearing the Tiger 110 dual seat, but some time later a slimmer 'sports' seat, as fitted to the Trophy models, appeared on T120s. The earlier type was covered in waterproof black 'Vynide' with thin white piping around the top edge. Possibly, adverse reaction to this seat in the USA prompted the change, but, in any event, later UK and US models were supplied with a narrower, shallower item more in keeping with the Bonneville image.

Also covered in black Vynide, most sports seats also featured grey trim around the lower edges, although there were also seats without the extra trim. For machines supplied to the US West Coast, passenger safety straps on seats were required by law and these were supplied as kits to be fitted by the importer or dealer.

The styling of the Bonneville's pressed steel cycle parts was probably the area which attracted most criticism. At the front of the machine, the deeply valanced front mudguard, shared with the Tiger 110 tourer, seemed wrong for a high-performance mount. The guard was mounted by means of a long stay doubling as a front wheel stand, running from its rear lower edge to the bottom of the fork legs. Two short strip-steel stays were riveted to the mudguard centre and attached higher up on the fork legs. The guard proved prone to cracking around this centre mounting, so, after engine number 021941, the stays were welded on rather than riveted.

All of the mudguard's edges were rolled and there was a raised longitudinal centre band onto which a pressed steel number plate was bolted near the front edge. Curiously, the plate was supplied on US models despite the fact that motorcycles in the 'States did not carry front numbers. Some dealers added logos or model names to the otherwise blank plate, so such an addition can be regarded as authentic on restored US models.

A Tangerine centre stripe was separated from the Pearl Grey ground colour by a gold pinstripe and finished just short of the leading and trailing edges of the guard, where it was squared-off by the pinstripe. As a general rule, when other Triumphs are fitted with rolled-edge mudguards, the centre stripe finishes short of the edge and is squared-off in this manner. If the mudguard edges are not rolled, the centre stripe is continued right up to, and even slightly over, the edge.

An all-welded steel petrol tank, carrying the famous Triumph grille badges and a chromed parcel rack, was the dominant piece of 'bodywork' on the new model. A four-gallon tank was used on UK and general export machines, while US machines got the three-gallon (Imperial measure) sports tank with a filler cap retaining chain, as found on the Trophy.

In all cases, colours were Pearl Grey for the upper half with Tangerine below, until Azure Blue appeared on some UK and general export machines later in the season. A chromed strip running along the waist of the tank divided the colours and another similar strip covered the raised longitudinal seam along its top. Rubber knee grips were fitted on both sizes of tank, although those fitted on US market tanks were

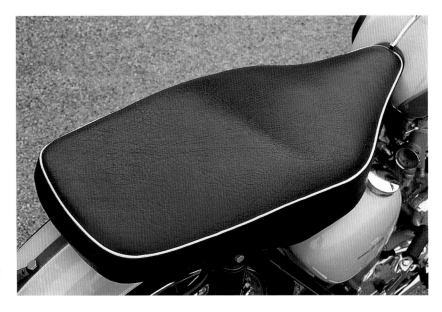

smaller and fitted over a plate screwed to the tank, rather than being fixed directly on the tank itself. Regardless of capacity, two petrol taps were fitted on either side of the tank at the rear.

The five-pint oil tank was mounted on the right side of the machine behind the carburettors. Initially finished in black on UK and general export models, the tank had Pearl Grey paintwork for the US, later adopted for UK models as well. A gold transfer about half-way up the side of the tank advised the owner of the correct oil level. Feed and scavenge pipes were situated on the lower front of the tank, the feed union incorporating a removable gauze filter. A tank-draining plug was sited roughly in the centre of its lower outside edge and a breather tube from the primary chaincase led into a vent high on the tank. For competition use a one-gallon oil tank was available,

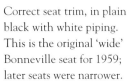

Correct seat trim, in plain black with white piping. This is the original 'wide' Bonneville seat for 1959; later seats were narrower.

Although it looks tiny, 'Bonneville 120' transfer is the correct type for tool box cover.

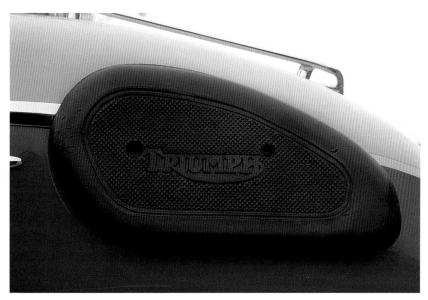

Triumph's famous grille tank badge straddles a chrome strip dividing the tank colours. UK knee-grip, as seen, screws directly to tank, whereas smaller US type presses on to mounting plates.

Rear lamp and number plate, showing centre stripe on mudguard finishing just short of rolled edge.

together with necessary modified fixings.

Opposite the oil tank on the left side was the combined battery carrier and tool box, which formed the other half of the air filter housing on the rest of the range. Like the oil tank, this was finished in either Pearl Grey or black depending on the destination of the machine and when during the year it was produced. Hinged straps secured the battery in the front portion of the box, while its rear section housed a comprehensive tool kit including a magneto spanner and clutch hub extractor as well as the usual range of spanners and screwdrivers. The cover was secured by a single large screw able to be readily loosened using a coin, and a gold 'Bonneville 120' transfer was applied centrally just above it.

The rear mudguard shared the front guard's colour scheme and rolled edges except at its concealed leading edge, where it had a straight-cut edge. It was bolted to the rear frame section, as was a tubular steel lifting handle located behind the left-side suspension unit's top mount. A pressed-steel rear number plate finished in black completed the rear end.

Electrics

Like many British manufacturers of the time, Triumph bought electrical components from Joseph Lucas Ltd in nearby Birmingham. Also, at the time of the Bonneville's launch, the preferred ignition system for a sports machine was the magneto with its adjustable spark timing, rather than coil ignition. The new Triumph had a flange-mounted Lucas K2F twin-cylinder magneto in the UK, with manual advance controlled from a lever on the left handlebar.

Auto-advance units to suit the K2F appeared later in the model year. US models got the K2FC Red Label competition-standard magneto, again with manual advance, although they too could be converted to auto advance later that year. Principally for the US market again, a racing specification magneto, the K2FR, was an option.

The magneto was located behind the cylinder block, held in place by three studs through its flange and secured by three special $\frac{5}{16}$in nuts accepting a smaller $\frac{1}{4}$in spanner size. The instrument's shaft protruded into the timing chest, where its pinion meshed with the inlet camshaft gear. The steel magneto pinion was pressed onto a taper on the magneto shaft and fastened by a nut which locked it onto the taper once ignition timing had been set. Ignition timing was set fully advanced with the piston at 39 degrees (or $\frac{7}{16}$in) before top dead centre (BTDC), while the magneto's contact-breaker points' gap was set at 0.012in, fully open. KLG FE100 or Lodge HLN sparking plugs were specified, gapped at 0.020in, though the parts book also listed Champion N3s.

While the Thunderbird tourer's battery and coil ignition, lights and horn were powered from an AC alternator, the T120 retained the more antiquated dynamo DC system. Its positive-earth Lucas E3L dynamo was mounted by a securing strap to the front of the crankcase and located into a forward extension of the inner timing chest cast integrally with the right-side crankcase half. Driven by a pinion meshing with the exhaust cam, the six-volt unit produced 60W. Output was controlled by a Lucas RB107 combined regulator and cut-out, replaced after engine number 024137 by the more effective and robust 37725H.

The battery charged by this system was a black-cased Lucas PU7E/9, of six-volt, 12 amp-hour rating. All lighting, plus the horn, ran direct from this conventional lead acid battery. Mounted in the headlamp nacelle and operated by a spring-loaded push button in unit with the dipswitch on the left handlebar, the Lucas HF1441 horn was adjustable by means of a screw on its rear. Overall, wiring on the early Bonnevilles was fairly simple. A fabric-covered main harness served all components with connections made by male and female brass bullet-connectors.

The 7in Lucas headlamp dipped to the left for UK roads, but US models had straight-dipping bulbs. Bulbs were pre-focus 30/24W for the UK, 35/35W for general export and yellow 36/36W for France, as required at that time. A 3W pilot bulb and holder were also provided. Turning the two small screws on either side of the headlamp retaining ring effected beam adjustment.

Lucas also supplied the ammeter, kill switch and lighting switch. At the rear of the machine, a lamp was fitted on the top portion of the pressed steel number plate, its red lens incorporating reflectors and housing a 6v 6/18W combined stop and tail lamp bulb. A spring-loaded switch, connected in series with the battery negative terminal, activated the stop lamp filament from the foot brake pedal's action.

Instruments

A Smiths Chronometric 120mph speedometer with light was driven by a cable from a pinion on the end of the gearbox layshaft. Sharing space with it in the headlamp nacelle was a black-faced Lucas ammeter, the only other instrument fitted to the standard Bonneville. Also on top of the nacelle were the lighting switch and ignition cut-out button. A 'Made in England' transfer was applied just below the steering damper knob, while a 'Bonneville 120' decal resided ahead of the damper and below the cut-out.

A rev counter was available in the list of performance parts and could be used with or without

Lucas K2FC competition magneto seen from both sides. Drive is from inlet camshaft gear via a pinion. Access to points on the other side is gained by turning serrated ring anti-clockwise to unthread it.

the dynamo fitted. If the dynamo was removed, as it might be for racing, the rev counter was driven by a cable from a special drive unit replacing it at the rear of the timing chest. Alternatively, if the dynamo was retained, a tachometer kit was available in the form of a timing cover assembly with a drive from the exhaust camshaft.

Nacelle and instruments detail on a 1959 model. 'Bonneville 120' transfer should be located forward of steering damper knob.

Chapter 3

Duplex frame, pre-unit engine: 1960-62

Despite answering popular demand, the Bon-neville was only a qualified success in its first year, especially in the USA, from where much of the impetus for its creation had come. The first bone of contention was the Tangerine and Pearl Grey colour scheme, apparently deemed too loud even in the USA. In the UK, adverse

reaction to the scheme caused the mid-season switch to a more conservative Pearl Grey and Royal Blue combination. Customers in the 'States had to put up with the original scheme, however, and through 1960 large numbers of left-over Tangerine and Grey 1959 models were still being marketed.

Duplex frame was the major new feature for 1960. This UK-market T120 dates from 1962, the year the grey-topped seat was introduced. Colours are Sky Blue and Silver.

Because of that, Triumph designated the new-look 1960 duplex-framed Bonneville for 1960 as the TR7 in America, to differentiate it from the unsold T120s. However, all engine numbers still carried the T120 prefix, since the TR7 code – which associated the twin-carburettor model with the popular sporty TR6 Trophy-Bird US models – was solely for the purpose of marketing and was only used in 1960. These machines were offered in TR7/A roadster and TR7/B off-road versions.

The early Bonneville's main problem in America had been its deeply valanced touring mudguards and the headlamp nacelle. For West Coast riders, the favoured look was the street scrambler, as exemplified by the TR6. Stateside owners who wanted their Bonnevilles to look as fast as they went junked the hated 'tinware'.

Even on the more traditional-minded home market, there was a feeling that the Bonneville looked a little too much like its touring Tiger 110. Triumph was to learn that if someone buys the top-of-the-range model, they want everyone to know about it at first glance!

Perhaps more importantly, given the sporting nature and performance of the Bonneville, high-speed handling of the 1959 model left something to be desired. The single downtube Tiger 110 frame was identified as the cause of high-speed weave and replaced after only one year of use on the T120.

So for the new season, the Bonneville moved away from its dated touring origins and began to acquire its own distinctive identity. The 1960

High-level exhausts, with slotted heat shields, on 1962 US T120C, in US-only colours of Flame and Silver Sheen. Duplex frame shows clearly in the angled view.

model was radically different from the previous year in several areas, and hereafter T120 development was to be continual. From engine number 029364 to 030424 and from D101 onwards, the revised model was set apart from the inaugural Bonneville by Triumph's new twin-downtube frame, changes to pressed-steel parts, and modifications to engine and electrics.

Engine

1960

Internally things stayed the same, but a few alterations to the engine casings accommodated the change to alternator electrics. With the disappearance of the dynamo came a new right-side crankcase half minus the mounting boss. On the left, a new primary chaincase cover bulged over the crankshaft-mounted alternator. Because of this bulkier cover, a new exhaust system was required. While this looked virtually identical to the previous system and was still of 1½in diameter, it featured a removable mute in the silencers.

In the 'States, the TR7B Scrambler sported high-level pipes with heat shields – to protect the rider's legs – and short silencers. TR7A roadsters also benefited from a tachometer driven from the exhaust camshaft. To accommodate this, the timing cover with a built-in drive take-off was fitted as standard and the familiar triangular Triumph patent plate relocated to a new position on the bulge housing the drive.

1961

On the 1961 engine (number D7727 onwards), change was restricted to a new cylinder head casting with vertical pillars bracing the outer cooling fins, to reduce ringing. Few changes to the engine were made for 1961, although there were gearbox revisions.

1962

Vibration was still the bugbear of the Bonneville and steps to address this problem were the only changes to the motor (number D15789 onwards) for 1962. Up until this year the crankshaft balance factor had been 50 per cent, but from engine number D15789 this was increased to 71 per cent.

Further efforts to tame the twin's vibrations were made from engine number D17043, when a new crankshaft assembly was introduced with a balance factor of 85 per cent. The new crank featured 'pear-shaped' webs and helped tame the vibes, but at the expense of throttle response.

Each of the two camshaft drive pinions now had three alternative keyways. Previously only available as optional performance parts, these wheels allowed much more accurate setting of the valve timing.

Fuel system & carburettors

1960

Although the Amal carburettors were initially the same as used in 1959, the remote float bowl was now mounted further forward, suspended on a threaded bar from a Metalastik anti-vibration bush on the rear head steady. The float bowl itself changed too: for 1960 a Type 14/624 replaced the earlier Type 14/617, but fuel frothing persisted. From engine number D5975, standard Amal Monoblocs with integral float bowls were fitted, which seemed to cure poor running at low revs.

1961

Following the fitting of standard Monoblocs, the previous year, no modifications to the fuel system were deemed necessary.

1962

The carburettors were unchanged, but the fuel tap arrangement was altered to allow one tap to feed both carburettors, meaning that the other functioned as a reserve tap. This was fine in theory, but in practice both taps needed to be turned on if the engine was to be given free rein. There were still no air filters fitted over the chromed bell mouths remaining on the 1¹⁄₁₆in Monoblocs.

Bolted-on sump guard and alloy straps holding cables to downtube are correct on T120C. Tachometer drive required a revised timing cover.

Change to non-chopped Monobloc carburettors came during 1960, but float bowl covers are still lockwired on 1962 T120C. Bracket on tank base is for absent tyre inflator.

Transmission

1960

Minor changes included an engine sprocket reduced from 24 to 22 teeth. With the clutch drum sprocket remaining at 43 teeth, slightly lower gearing resulted. The only other alteration was the revised primary drive cover.

1961

Still using the Slickshift outer cover, the gearbox received a couple of modifications for this year. During the 1961 season, needle-roller layshaft bearings replaced Oilite plain bushes. The gearbox main casing and its inner cover

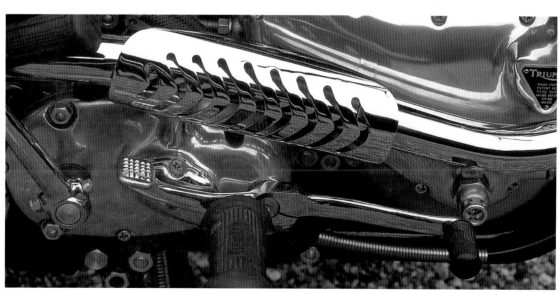

'Heel and toe' gearchange lever, seen on US T120C, was listed as a Triumph accessory in the USA.

were also modified to accept a larger thrust washer bearing at each end of the layshaft. With the gearbox still separate from the engine, the factory anchored and aligned it more firmly by doubling up the primary chain adjusters at the box's upper mount. The engine sprocket lost another tooth, going down from 22 to 21 teeth, and gearbox ratios were tweaked to lower gearing even more. A folding kick-start lever was now standard.

1962

Another year, and another change to the gearbox ratios, as Triumph strove to optimise the Bonneville's punchy mid-range pull with a slightly higher third gear.

Frame & rear suspension

1960

About the only similarity the new frame had with the 1959 version was the black-enamelled finish. Designed to cure handling deficiencies, the new frame was instantly recognisable by its twin front downtubes running from the steering head and forming the engine cradle under the crankcase.

Less obvious, but no less important, was the steeper steering angle of 67 degrees as opposed to 64½ degrees for the 1959 model. The intention was to improve steering and stability, and, with the new strengthened rear subframe, it was a marked improvement. The steering angle change reduced the wheelbase from 55¾in to 54½in.

Head-on view of a 1962 UK T120 shows how duplex-frame models retained the Bonneville's slim lines. Detail shows right-side rear wheel chain tension adjuster.

Duplex frame (facing page), still finished in black enamel, has twin front downtubes running from steering head and forming engine cradle under crankcase. Glossed fork gaiters were fastened at their lower ends only.

The new frame followed earlier practice by being in two sections (front and rear) and having lugged and brazed construction, but the method of joining the two parts was now different. At the top, the rear-section bolted join was as before but, at the bottom, the rear subframe was shortened and attached to a substantial lug at the base of the central vertical tube.

Possibly to ease assembly, there was no lower tank rail on the new frame, and front tank mounting points were now fixed on the twin downtubes with a single mounting for the rear of the tank incorporated into the rear of the top frame tube. The omission of the extra tube proved mistaken as breakages at the head lug occurred in use, mainly in the fierce proving ground of American dirt and desert racing. From engine number D1563, a revised front frame incorporated a strengthening lower frame rail and dealers subsequently fitted it to many earlier machines.

Naturally, new engine plates were required. At the front, the new mounting was a one-piece structure with its side plates joined at the top. A new rear head-steady consisted of a flat plate running from the top frame rail to one of the main head studs, and it also held the rod from which the remote float bowl was suspended.

At the rear, the new subframe was substantially different from its predecessor. Of all-welded construction, it now had the rear footrest hangers welded rather than bolted to it, and the rear loop extended further back to provide support for the rear mudguard.

The swinging arm remained unchanged, as it would until the advent of the unit-construction Bonnevilles in 1963. The rear brake pedal now had its previously epic length trimmed a little. The centre and prop stands remained unchanged until it was realised that with the steeper fork angle and stiffer fork springs, the prop stand was now too short. Mid-season, it was replaced by a longer version.

1961 & 1962

The change to frames with lower tank rails was accompanied by another alteration of the steering angle, to 65 degrees, to further enhance handling. This frame continued into 1962, when the only other change was uprating of the Girling rear suspension units, which gained stiffer (145lb/in) springs as standard.

Steering & front suspension

1960

Although sharing many components with the 1959 fork, the 1960 version was significantly different. Two-way damping was the main improvement for the rider, but there were many more subtle

changes for restorers to be wary of. The fork sliders were still finished in black enamel, but with new mounting points for the mudguard stays cast into their trailing edges. Each fork now contained 150cc of SAE 20W30 oil, and the right-side slider incorporated a lug on the inside to anchor the brake plate.

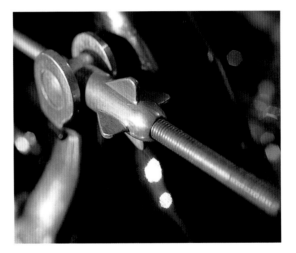

TR6 Trophy fork top yoke was adopted for 1960, when chromed headlamp shell replaced the nacelle.

Details on 1962 models show correct 'rocket' rear brake adjuster and brake light switch arrangement.

Wider Dunlop WM3 rear wheel rim was introduced for 1961.

A striking visual change took place at the top of the fork: gone was the unloved nacelle, replaced by combined fork shrouds and headlamp brackets in sheet steel and finished in black. Below them, glossy black rubber gaiters were clamped at their lower ends to the tops of the fork sliders.

The same bottom yoke as in 1959 gripped the new-look fork, but the top yoke was changed to the type used on the TR6 Trophy. Finished as before in black, it featured integral handlebar clamps with detachable tops, which were slightly raised and pulled back compared to the 1959 T120 'bar position. The friction damper's lower back-plate was now anchored to the frame without a bolt. North American TR7/A and TR7/B models had high handlebars while UK and general export Bonnevilles had the lower type.

Controls were similar to the previous year but the ignition cut-out was now fitted just to the right of the steering damper knob. Also, the magneto advance lever disappeared from the left-side on UK models as they now had an auto advance unit like American machines.

1961 & 1962

After the major redesign of 1960, no further changes to the forks and handlebars were made in the next two years.

Wheels, brakes & tyres

1960

These aspects of the Bonneville were little altered, although it is interesting to note that the great majority of machines supplied to the

USA were fitted with the more expensive QD rear hub which was specified as an optional extra in other markets. The rear hub sprocket now had 43 teeth.

1961 & 1962

While the front wheel's size remained unaltered, the rear wheel got a 4.00-section Dunlop Universal rear tyre in 1961, along with a wider WM3-18 rim to accommodate it. The front and rear brakes were improved by new backing plates and fully-floating brake shoes.

Seat & bodywork

1960

To go with the all-new frame was a new dual seat. It was, in fact, from the factory's touring range and rather more generously upholstered than the 1959 Bonneville's backside-numbing perch. Finished in black textured vinyl with white piping round the upper edge and a black lower trim strip, the seat was used on both UK and US machines. The seat was bolted to the frame rather than hinged, as it would be in later years.

The fuel tank's mounting changed to suit the new frame. It now rested on three rubbers, two at the front and one at the rear, and was secured by a chromed steel top strap bolted to the frame at the rear and pulled tight by a draw bolt running almost vertically through the lower frame lug on the steering head. A protective rubber strip under it covered the centre seam, while a rubber 'horseshoe' wrapped around the frame top-tube prevented side-to-side tank movement. After engine number D104, the factory supplied custom-made rubber blocks for this purpose. The chromed parcel rack and filler cap were still fitted as before. Once again, UK models got the larger four-gallon tank while US versions had the smaller three-gallon (Imperial measure) vessel.

Colours for the new model were Pearl Grey and Azure Blue for both UK and US versions, with the top half of the tank in grey and the lower half in blue, separated by a gold line.

Mudguarding was revamped. Gone were the old heavy steel touring guards, hated by young bloods on both sides of the Atlantic, to be replaced by an alloy front blade and a much slimmer steel rear guard without the deep valances. Both had straight leading and trailing edges, with their blue centre stripes going right to the edge of the grey guards rather than stopping just short as before. The gold lining on the mudguards was retained and, following on from late 1959 models, the oil tank and battery box kept their Pearl Grey finish.

Drive-side view of 1962 UK Bonneville, which has a larger fuel tank than the US version. Bulge at front of primary case accommodates alternator.

Left-hand machine is a 1960 TR7B, the name given to genuine 1960 models in the USA. For that year, unsold 1959 models were still on sale, tagged T120, and the TR7B model code was used for just one season. On the right is a 1962 US-market T120R, complete with high pipes.

A 1962 US T120C, still with parcel rack. Front number plates were redundant in the USA and often decorated by dealers or owners.

A passenger grab strap was added to US models to comply with West Coast regulations.

Fuel tank mounting changed in 1960, with the tank resting on three rubbers and held down by a central strap. Front tank mounting bosses are prominent on smaller US tank.

1961

The seat stayed the same, as did the mudguards except for their new colours. But the petrol tank, oil tank and tool box all received attention, mostly as a result of problems with vibration-induced fractures on their predecessors. Both UK and US versions of the petrol tank were strengthened at the nose and a new stainless steel retaining strap finally put a stop to breakages of this component. The new strap was available in two lengths to suit the differing sizes of home market and US tanks. New colours for the petrol tank were Sky Blue for the top half, complemented by Silver on the lower part. As before, a gold line separated the two colours.

A new oil tank in Silver featured stronger anti-vibration mountings, and from engine number D9660 the tool box got similar treatment. Mudguards followed the new colour scheme with Silver as their main colour and a gold-lined, Sky Blue centre stripe going right up to the edge of each guard.

1962

The most obvious change for 1962, at least on UK and general export machines, was the new two-tone seat. Exactly the same as before in terms of shape,

base and mounting, the new seat featured a grey top separated by white piping from black sides and a grey lower trim strip.

Colours remained the same as 1961 for UK and general export models, with the exception of oil tanks and tool boxes reverting to black. US machines, however, got a Silver Sheen and Flame scheme. Petrol tanks on US machines had a Flame top half with Silver Sheen lowers, with the familiar gold lining separating them. Oil tanks and tool boxes were finished in Silver Sheen early in the season, before following the UK machines and becoming black later in the year. Mudguards were Silver Sheen with a Flame stripe and gold lining.

Electrics

1960
Magneto ignition was retained throughout the lifespan of the pre-unit Bonneville models, although from 1960 UK machines received Lucas K2F auto-advance units which gave 30 degrees of spark advance variation. US machines continued with K2FC units.

All Bonnevilles switched to alternator electrics for 1960 when a Lucas RM15 six-volt alternator was mounted on the drive-side end of the crankshaft. This charged an identical battery to that fitted in the previous year, via a rectifier converting current from AC to DC and an ammeter mounted in the all-new chromed QD headlamp shell. With the disappearance of the unpopular nacelle, the headlamp switch was relocated to just below the nose of the dual seat on the right side.

At the same time, the horn was relocated to the frame crossbar beneath the seat.

Apart from the redirected wires to the light switch, the main difference to the wiring loom was the quick-release plug and socket connection to the headlamp shell. This featured on all Bonneville models until 1963, but was dropped due to problems with the plug loosening. Despite the new shell,

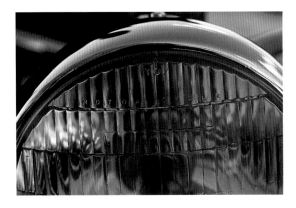

Unvalanced mudguards introduced in 1960 are slimmer and no longer have rolled edges. Front stays for the front 'guards arrived in 1960, staying unchanged for the life of the 'pre-unit' models. Stripes on this 1962 UK model correctly extend to the edge of the 'guards.

Clutch lever shares handlebar mounting with headlamp main and dip switch. Genuine Lucas motorcycle headlamp glass enhances originality.

Electrical details show 1960-62 positions of lighting switch (above), under the nose of the seat, and of horn (right), hidden under the seat – not the best location to be audible. Lucas ammeter (below) as used in duplex-frame T120 headlamp shells.

headlamp and pilot bulb wattage remained the same. At the rear, the stop and tail lamp was unchanged, but a new Type 6A brake light switch appeared.

1961

In an effort to reduce the incidence of bulb failures, particularly common at high engine speeds, a lower-output alternator was specified. Yet another (Type 22B) brake light switch was tried, but otherwise the electrics were largely as before.

1962

When the American off-road variant was designated T120C for 1962, this machine was fitted with the more waterproof 'Wader' version of the Lucas K2FC auto-advance magneto.

A new Lucas RM19 alternator appeared, although retaining the low-output stator to minimise bulb failure and overcharging of the battery. The horn was changed to a Type H8 and the rectifier was also renewed.

Instruments

1960-62

New for 1960 was a revised Smiths Chronometric speedometer calibrated up to 120mph. As before, this had its own internal lamp, odometer and trip recorder. US models also benefited from a matching rev counter placed to the left of the speedo and driven from the exhaust cam on the right-hand side of the machine. Off-road B variants had only the speedometer.

Chapter 4

Early unit construction: 1963-65

After all the work Triumph had put into development of the Bonneville since its launch in 1959, some people were surprised that Meriden's range-topper was virtually all-new for 1963. Perhaps it should not have been such a shock. After all, the 350 and 500cc range had employed unit construction of the engine and gearbox for several years and it was inevitable that the larger twins would follow suit. As unit construction made for easier factory assembly, it was bound to come for that reason alone.

The first unit construction Bonneville started a period of continuous development intended to keep the T120 at the top of an increasingly competitive

Major redesign for 1963 brought the new unit-construction engine and another new frame, but Bonneville's essential character was retained. This is a US T120R.

Robert Sullivan's immaculate 1964 US T120R. For this year, larger 1⅛in 389 Amal Monobloc carburettors were used, with suitably enlarged intakes.

market. But for the restorer, the non-stop nature of Bonneville development from 1963 onward means careful research is often necessary to determine which features are correct for a particular machine. Many revisions were implemented as soon as possible on the production line and not necessarily confined to the end or beginning of a model year. The pace and extent of change was about to hot up.

As the T120 was so popular and already well on its way to legendary status, Triumph was careful to retain strong visual links with the past. Although the unit construction model differed from its predecessor in many ways, it was immediately recognisable as a Bonneville.

Engine

1963

The first year of unit construction, from engine number DU 101, saw wholesale change of the power plant, but some components from the old pre-unit motor were either retained or used in modified form. Engines were stamped with the prefix T120R (for road models) or T120C (for off road or scrambler models).

Starting from the top of the unit engine, an all-new cylinder head casting was the first important change. Its most significant feature was an extra central ⁵⁄₁₆in holding down bolt, and rearrangement of the eight ⅜in main bolts to provide more metal around the valve seats to prevent cracks forming, an all-too-frequent occurrence with eight-bolt alloy heads. Improved sealing and less likelihood of warping were other benefits, as was the scope to increase valve sizes in the future. The new casting also featured deeper finning and the splayed inlets with their threaded inserts for the carburettor mounts no longer carried unmachined T110 bosses.

The unpolished rocker boxes now carried horizontal finning and slightly shallower inspection caps with cross-slots and milled edges. Spring-steel clips bore on the serrated edges to reduce the chances of the caps loosening and being lost as a result of inevitable parallel-twin vibration. Valve sizes remained unchanged for the time being, while the exhaust pipes were slightly revised to fit the new motor. Silencers were altered to suit revised mounting positions and received longer internal baffles, resulting in a slightly heavier and less sleek appearance. High pipes, as fitted to the off-road T120C models in the USA, were only changed very slightly, retaining their elegant look.

Under the new cylinder head, a revised 'nine stud' cast-iron barrel contained the previous 8.5:1 pistons and connecting rods. The new block was essentially unchanged at the crankcase joint, and so could be fitted to earlier bottom ends.

All-new main castings, of course, were used for the bottom end. However, Triumph designers went out of their way to maintain the link with the old model and emphasise that the unit construction machine was still very much a Bonneville. Accordingly, the styling of the integral gearbox housing closely followed the shape of the old separate unit, and the overall look did not change much. Internally, a new crankshaft was fitted, with the flywheel retaining bolts secured with Loctite fluid rather than the serrated lock washers previously employed. The crankshaft's end-fed timing-side nose now turned in an efficient oil seal in the timing cover rather than a phosphor-bronze bush, so pressure was better maintained over high mileage.

Under the new cover, which retained the distinctive triangular shape and patent plate, other changes took place. Wider-section timing pinions now drove the revised camshafts (E4819 inlet and E4855 exhaust), and the exhaust shaft now had provision for rev-counter drive at its drive-side end, where a cable take-off was incorporated into the casting. As the new model dispensed with a magneto in favour of coil ignition, the exhaust camshaft also drove the twin contact breakers located at its timing-side end. A chromed steel cover held by two Phillips-head screws provided access to the points.

A new plunger oil pump featured reversed chambers, meaning that the feed chamber was

Unit engine's revised cylinder head with nine holding-down bolts: unmachined T110 inlet stub castings have gone.

If a rev counter is fitted on a 1963 model, its drive comes directly off the drive-side end of the exhaust camshaft.

now on the right. At the same time, the oil pressure indicator was moved from the outer face of the timing cover to a new position facing forward on the leading edge.

On the drive side of the unit, the primary chaincase was no longer pierced by the mounting for the rider's footrest. On the surface of the new outer casting, a flash bearing the cast-in Triumph logo extended rearward from the alternator bulge. Inside the case were revised and strengthened clutch and primary drive arrangements.

Special performance parts listed for 1963 were numerous. Among them were roller main bearings and 8.5:1 pistons machined to accept valves increased in diameter by ³⁄₃₂in, together with valve seats to suit the increased sizes and adaptors to allow the fitting of 1⅛in carburettors. To suit these larger Type 389 Amal carburettors, there was also an Amal 14/624 remote float chamber.

Other extras were E3134-profile inlet and exhaust cams with followers to suit, close-ratio gears (with special speedometer drive gear) and heavy-duty clutch springs. Larger 19in wheel rims front and rear were also listed together with MZ41 racing brake linings, racing handlebars, competition number holders and a rev counter with combined speedo and tacho mounting bracket.

1964

Minor revisions, rather than wholesale changes, were made for 1964 starting at engine number DU 5825. Following the previous year's cylinder head redesign, the opportunity was taken to increase

Great view of 1965 TT Special shows single downtube of new frame introduced in 1963. Colours are Pacific Blue and Silver. This is another beauty from the Sullivan collection in New England.

valve sizes, inlet diameter going up to 1¹⁹⁄₃₂in and exhaust to 1⁷⁄₁₆in.

In the bottom end, lateral alignment of the crankshaft was no longer achieved by pulling up against the drive-side main bearing. Location was now at the timing side, where the clamping washer (E3300) fitted behind the timing pinion was dispensed with and a new gear with a longer shoulder behind its teeth introduced. A revised crankcase casting permitted the oil filter screen in the sump area to be larger.

The breather at the drive-side end of the inlet camshaft now vented via a T-piece into the oil tank froth tower and to the atmosphere by a pipe running along the right side of the rear mudguard.

1965

As in the previous year, improvements from the start of 1965, with engine number DU13375, were fairly minor and in the nature of refinements rather than extensive redesigns. The right-side crankcase gained a threaded drilling in a boss behind the cylinder block through which a special tool could be inserted to determine top dead centre when it engaged with a notch in the fly-wheel. A new oil pressure relief valve dispensed with the indicator, which had been identified as a source of oil leaks.

In the cylinder head, aluminium exhaust stubs were used from engine number DU22682, in the hope (vain as it turned out) of reducing the incidence of stubs loosening. Champion sparking plugs and caps also became standard equipment. T120R models received restyled exhaust down-pipes, swept back more and carrying welded-on ears near the bottom bend to attach a chromed strap, which ran between the pipes to brace them. UK models continued with the long resonator-type silencers, but US T120Rs got shorter mufflers with straight-through internals.

Fuel system & carburettors

1963

The 1¹⁄₁₆in Amal Monoblocs were retained for 1963, though the fuel lines changed from black material to clear plastic. But there were still no starting chokes and no air filtration was provided on UK models. Later in the season, some US machines gained a one-piece filter attached to the frame and connected to the carburettor intakes via rubber adaptors. It would be another five years before UK models were afforded such a luxury as standard, although separate 'pancake' type filters were available as optional extras.

1964

To achieve more even slow-running, a flexible balance pipe now linked the carburettor inlet

Carburettors and air filter on 1965 T120C TT Special. Note grommets on tool box cover where lighting switch would normally reside.

One-piece air filter was standard for the USA, but only available on request on the home market.

Footrests were mounted on rear engine plates for 1965. TT Specials had no pillion footrests.

standard set-up now being 19-tooth gearbox and 46-tooth rear wheel sprockets.

1964

The unit gearbox now had a new seal around the kick-start shaft and, while the gearbox output sprocket remained at 19 teeth on UK and US road models, the Stateside T120C and newly-launched TT Special competition machine had an 18-tooth sprocket. The sleeve gear splines on which the sprocket engaged were widened, mainly to ease assembly at the factory.

1965

A thrust washer was fitted to the mainshaft, along with a shorter kick-start ratchet pinion sleeve, to prevent the kick-start from 'hanging up' so readily. On the primary drive side, Armstrong cork clutch linings were now specified as standard and a longer alternator cable nut prevented the primary chain chafing the cable.

Frame & rear suspension

1963

The frame was totally new, attempting to address some of the handling deficiencies and uncomfortable vibration for which the duplex-framed Bonne-ville had become known. Still in two sections, the new structure was a single downtube design, but with significant improvements over the old version. The downtube was now considerably larger in diameter than the 1959 frame at 1⅜in, while the steering head casting, which retained the same 65-degree steering angle as used in 1962, was a lot more substantial.

Again, the frame featured a bracing lower frame rail under the top tube, which carried a flat plate on which the front of the petrol tank rested, held by rubber-bushed bolts. Under the engine, the frame split into a double cradle, but at the base of the central vertical tube a new swinging arm mounting lug, integral with the rear engine mounting, stiffened the frame considerably. The swinging arm itself was also totally new, being stouter and stiffer than its predecessor.

For this year only, the footrests bolted directly to lugs on the frame just below the engine, and the brake pedal pivoted on the left-side rear engine plate. As had become normal practice, the US-market T120C off-roader had the benefit of a protective steel 'bash plate' bolted to the frame under the front of the engine.

At the rear, a new subframe carried the Girling shock absorbers, which were now rated at 145lb/in for the UK and general export markets or 100lb/in for the USA. Passenger footrests now mounted on plates bolted to the rear subframe, which doubled as silencer mountings. The combination of the

manifolds. Amal 389 instruments replaced the 376 units, with choke size up to 1⅛in. US models wore the long 'pancake' style air filter as standard.

Transmission

1963

Inside the primary drive cover was a completely new ⅜in duplex chain, driven by a 29-tooth engine sprocket. Because the gearbox could no longer be moved relative to the engine, tensioning of the chain was provided by a rubber-covered blade bearing on its lower run and adjustable from the outside of the case.

The clutch had always been at the limit of its ability to transmit the 650cc twin's torque, so for 1963 the unit models gained an extra friction plate, bringing the total up to six. Stronger clutch springs were also fitted, and, to cope with the heavier action that resulted, there was a ball-and-ramp clutch-lifting mechanism, with three balls installed in the new gearbox outer cover.

The cast-iron clutch basket was another all-new part, with 58 teeth to suit the duplex chain on its outer circumference. A three-vane clutch shock absorber replaced the previous four-vane type and now had a bronze thrust washer to reduce clutch rattle. At the rear of the primary case, which now had 350cc oil capacity, a tube with an integral metering jet conveyed lubricant to the final drive chain.

Despite now being within the main engine casting, the gearbox was little changed internally. Apart from the revised clutch-lifting mechanism, the main alteration was that a variety of layshaft pinions became available to adapt the speedometer drive to suit different overall gearing, the new, more rigid chassis and the unit construction motor did much to diminish the Bonneville's reputation as a less-than-perfect handler.

1964

Frame changes were minimal, consisting of a revised oil tank support and the relocation of the rider's footrest mounting to the rear engine plates rather than directly onto frame lugs as before. The centre stand also gained a stronger tang, brazed to the main stand rather than attached by means of a cotter pin.

1965

A modified prop stand lug reduced the angle of lean when the stand was used on a camber, a problem that would have been exacerbated by the increase in the fork length that year. Slight modification of the rear subframe allowed the swinging arm spindle to be fitted from the right rather than the left. Under the lower tank rail, a new bracket provided the horn location.

The rear brake rod's operating arm was now moved inside the left-side rear engine plate. This allowed a flat brake cam lever (W1466) to replace the offset arm (W1487) used before. The existing straight rod was retained.

The new centre stand pivot bolts had tab washers to prevent them slackening. The battery box bushes received steel inserts to prevent over-tightening of the anti-vibration rubbers.

Steering & front suspension

1963

Although the front fork itself was unchanged, a new top yoke casting appeared for 1963. Drilled to accept separate, rubber-bushed handlebar clamps, it was again finished in black enamel. New fork gaiters appeared, fashioned from a less glossy material than the previous year, although still only attached at their lower ends.

At the same time, the handlebar tubing was reduced in diameter to the industry norm of ⅞in, with shims in the clamps which could still accept 1in 'bars if desired. As usual, UK models wore low 'bars and US versions high ones. Controls were adapted to fit the new size of handlebars, but the layout was unchanged except for the disappearance of the ignition cut-out, and throttles operated via two separate cables without the previous splitter-box. The handlebar grips were now plastic Amal items with a chequered finish, replacing the 'Triumph' embossed rubber grips.

1964

This was probably the most significant area of change for 1964. All-new forks with external springs now lent the Bonneville's front end a more

sporty, purposeful air. The springs were located at the top by the underside of the lower yoke and at the bottom in larger slider caps which carried double lipped oil seals to retain the damping oil, the amount of which increased to 190cc per leg. The tops of the forks were still enclosed by sheet metal shrouds doubling as headlamp brackets, but the friction steering damper now gained an inner rubber bush to combat a tendency for it to slacken off in use. The larger diameter external springs meant that the protective rubber gaiters also became more substantial and, for the first time, they were secured top and bottom. For the US market, an optional extra was a twin-pull throttle twist grip.

1965

The Bonneville's forks were completely reworked for 1965, while retaining the overall appearance of the older front end. This has caused a few odd-looking and odd-handling machines to be produced

External fork springs, new for 1964, are concealed by gaiters that – unlike those of previous seasons – are now clamped at the top as well as the bottom. 'Made in England' transfer on frame downtube was applied by the factory only from 1971, but is often seen on restored machines from earlier production.

Details of handlebar controls on 1964 T120R. Twin-cable throttle and thinner plastic handgrips, were new for 1963.

1964

Rim and tyre sizes remained unchanged for 1964 on either side of the Atlantic, although there is evidence that Avon Speedmaster tyres replaced Dunlops on some UK machines.

1965

New for 1965 were grease retaining rings and felt washers, while the optional QD rear wheel made the change from taper roller to ball race bearings.

Seat & bodywork

1963

A hinged, rather than bolted-down, seat retained the look of earlier seats and was finished with a grey top with white piping round the edge, black sides and a grey lower trim band. American models arriving on the West Coast also had the usual passenger strap.

For 1963, the previous year's front mudguard and stays were retained. Colour was now Alaskan White with a gold centre stripe separated from the main colour by black pinstriping.

The new rear subframe dictated a new rear mudguard, although it was similar in appearance to the previous year's version, with a raised central ridge. Both mudguards had plain unrolled leading and trailing edges and shared the same colour scheme. Following the general rule for plain mudguards, their gold centre stripes continued over the ends of the guards.

With the exception of revised mountings to fit the new frame, the three-gallon US sports petrol tank and four-gallon home market version were little different. The rear tank mounting was now through a flat tab protruding from the rear of the tank, secured by a rubber-bushed screw threaded into a tapped hole in the frame. Colour scheme was a rather uninspired all-over Alaskan White and the tank retained the familiar grille badges. The smaller sports tank retained clip-on knee-grip rubbers, but the larger tank got much thinner glued-on rubber knee-pads covering a greater area of the tank. Underneath, both tanks were recessed to accommodate new twin ignition coils.

A revised oil tank appeared for 1963, dictated by the redesigned frame. Its filler cap and froth tower were now concealed by the hinged seat, forcing the oil instruction transfers out into the open at the top of the tank.

On the other side of the machine, a new cover carrying the ignition and lighting switch followed the curved line of the seat. Both the oil tank and the left-side cover were finished in black, as were the frame, engine plates, stands and mudguard stays, although the mudguard stays were stove-enamelled rather than spray-painted. Transfers remained unchanged apart from the relocated

when owners inadvertently fit the wrong forks for their machine. An inch of extra travel was afforded to the 1965 Bonneville by increasing the length of the stanchions, sliders and internal damping sleeves.

All-new sliders were machined in one piece and necessitated a new wheel spindle. The rubber fork gaiters now had sharper, less rounded and closer pitched folds, and were of larger diameter to accommodate the external springs. Softer and slightly longer fork springs were also fitted, while the steering damper was strengthened at its lower end. Although similar at first glance, the upper fork shrouds now featured slightly longer headlamp supports to afford more vertical adjustment of the light itself. For the US market, a slightly revised handlebar shape aimed to give a more comfortable riding position.

Wheels, brakes & tyres

1963

In the UK, wheel and tyre sizes were changed for 1963, there now being 18in rims front and rear. But in the USA they remained as before. At the front, a chromed WM2 rim laced to a full-width, silver-finished, iron hub wore a ribbed 3.25 x 18 Dunlop tyre. At the rear, a black pressed-steel hub was mated to a WM3 rim with a 3.50 x18 Dunlop Universal tyre. The brakes were unchanged and the QD rear wheel remained an option.

instructions, although the colour of lettering changed from gold to black during the year.

1964

The seat on all Bonnevilles remained unchanged, but there were some mudguard and tank updates. To suit the new forks, the front mudguard's centre brace received some attention, partly to allow the same part to be used with wheels of different diameters. By now, the front guard had reverted to being steel, except on US competition variants (see Chapter 6) which had polished alloy guards. A bracket providing mounting points for the two upper mudguard stays was attached to the top of the fork sliders. Using different plates here meant that the mudguard could be raised or lowered to accommodate various wheel diameters and mudguard heights. A tubular brace running over the top of the guard provided rigidity, replacing the flat brace previously employed. Colours for the year were Alaskan White with a gold centre strip delineated with black pinstriping.

The black oil tank, once again rubber-bushed, gained a drain plug and a new support at the bottom. As previously mentioned, the crankcase breather was now linked to the froth tower of the oil tank, which also had its own large-bore breather tube running back along the right side of the rear mudguard. A new chainguard, finished in black, slightly increased chain enclosure.

Petrol tanks retained the same part number as the previous year, but there was a significant change in finish. Gone was the familiar horizontal separation of the two colours on the tank, dividing it roughly into upper and lower halves. Instead, for 1964 the Gold upper colour covered about three quarters of the tank. The Alaskan White lower colour followed the lower edge of the tank badge before dropping down the side of the tank following the line of the knee grips, then finishing about halfway along the tank's lower edge. A black pinstripe separated the two main colours. Tank transfers remained in black, although the 'Made in England' box shrank and gained a Gold ground to match the tank.

1965

The hinged dual seat remained the same, but some were finished – for the US market at least – in all-black vinyl as well as the familiar two-tone grey

Drive-side view of 1963 US T120R in appropriate period setting. Alaskan White was the colour that year in both the UK and the USA.

Timing-side angle of 1964 US T120R in that season's colours of Gold and Alaskan White. Unit-construction engine's longer kick-start lever and unsightly but accurate oil tank transfer are clearly visible.

Purposeful views of a pair of US-market T120C TT Specials. Neither machine has lighting, but exhaust systems differ: Alaskan White 1963 machine has straight-through pipes, while Pacific Blue 1965 example has TT track racing pipes tucked in tightly under frame bottom rails. Note also, on the later bike, how rear brake rod passes through the shock absorber, a change introduced for 1965.

When an unwanted tank-top parcel rack was removed, fixing holes could be filled with blanking rubbers available from dealers. These two US machines are a 1963 T120R (with rack) and a 1965 T120C TT Special (without rack).

Chrome trim on tank side remained for 1963 (above) despite single colour scheme, but the section rearward of the badge disappeared thereafter (right). Latter view, of a 1965 tank, shows revised frame mounting on unit-construction models.

and black scheme. Apart from the TT Special, all Bonneville models for 1965 had steel mudguards front and rear, finished in Silver with a Pacific Blue centre stripe and gold pinstriping. Petrol tank paintwork followed the same pattern as 1964, but the colours were Pacific Blue over Silver with gold pinstriping.

Electrics

1963

Radical change also swept through the ignition system, consigning the magneto to the same fate as the dynamo. The six-volt alternator was retained and the battery now supplied power for the two Lucas MA6 ignition coils under the fuel tank. The alternator also incorporated an energy transfer coil to enable the machine to be started even if the battery was discharged. An emergency position on the ignition switch brought this extra coil into play if required. Ignition contact breaker points, with their attendant capacitors and an auto-advance unit giving a range of 12 degrees, were neatly housed under an inspection cover on the timing cover.

The wiring harness continued to be fabric-clad as before, but a short section of plastic sleeving now protected it where it passed through the fork yokes towards the headlamp. A non-QD Lucas 7in headlamp in a chromed shell replaced the previous unit, but retained the Lucas 2AR ammeter in the top and bulb wattage stayed at 30/24W. Charging by the alternator was via a rectifier and the system included a single 25-amp fuse. The Lucas 564 combined stop/tail light was as before, but a new, plunger-type stop light switch was relocated to the pressed steel chainguard, operated by brake rod movement. The same 8H horn as in 1962 was used, but it was now mounted in front of the battery on a welded-on bracket. As previously mentioned, lighting and ignition switches were installed in the left side panel, with the ignition switch below the lighting switch.

1964

No significant changes were made to the ignition system for 1964, save that the US T120C and TT Specials featured only 10 degrees of advance.

The only change of any note in the UK was the new pull-for-on rear brake light switch, positioned further back than before on the chainguard. In America, the off-road T120C now had a Lucas S55 cut-out switch on the handlebars.

1965

In the UK, changes were limited to moving the horn from its muffled under-seat position to a more sensible location under the front of the fuel tank. The wiring loom was modified accordingly. In the US, a larger Lucas L679 stop and tail light was fitted, but it retained the existing pressed steel number plate.

Instruments

1963

There was still no rev counter fitted as standard to UK models, although the drive facility from the end of the exhaust cam was present and the instrument was available as an option. If fitted, the cable took a perilous route round the outside of the left-side exhaust pipe before bending back inwards and upwards to meet up with the rev counter itself. In the USA a tachometer was original equipment. In all markets the speedometer was a Smiths 140mph Chronometric instrument.

1964

Both tachometer and speedometer were changed for 1964. Smiths magnetic instruments replaced the previous Chronometrics and the speedometer was now calibrated to 125mph. Both clocks were mounted on a common bracket, insulated from vibration by Metalastik bushes.

1965

A rev counter was now standard on road models for all markets, but some US T120C variants, which wore only speedometers, were supplied with German VDO instruments. On machines so equipped, a matching VDO tachometer was supplied on request.

Business-like rear end of 1963 TT Special with no number plate

Twin dials on a 1963 T120R. Rev counter was standard in the USA at this time, but still optional for UK buyers. Headlamp was no longer a quick-release type in 1963.

Rev counter was the sole instrument fitted to 1965 TT Special.

Chapter 5

Peak years for the T120: 1966-70

From 1966, the Bonneville went through a bewildering series of changes, often implemented without respect for strict model years. Revisions were made as soon as they could be effected on the production line. For a comprehensive listing of every detail change, careful perusal of the parts book for the year in question is recommended. An ever-increasing percentage of Bonneville output crossed the Atlantic, so more of the changes reflected demand and needs in the US market.

One year stands out: significant improvements made for 1968, particularly to the engine, have led many to regard this as a vintage year for the Bonneville. This year was also notable for being the first since 1960 in which no off-road variant of the Bonneville was offered in North America: the 1967 TT Specials, dealt with in the next chapter, were the last off-road competition T120s.

Also often regarded as a high point of Bonneville development, 1970 was the last year before problems within the parent BSA Group began to have a deleterious effect on Triumph's product.

US-market T120R in Alaskan White and Grenadier Red. Thinner tank knee-grip rubbers, grey handlebar grips and absence of tank parcel rack identify this as a 1966 model. 'Made in England' transfer on downtube is a restorer's addition.

Engine

1966

Major changes included a new crankshaft. Despite shedding 2½lbs in weight, the new crankshaft retained the familiar 85 per cent balance factor. This was achieved by removing metal from the edges of the flywheel, giving it a stepped profile.

As shown in the 1966 (September 1965) parts book, a 1⅛in shouldered roller main bearing (E2879) replaced the ballrace at the drive side and as a result, lateral location of the crankshaft reverted to the timing side with the re-introduction of the clamping washer (E3300) between the new mainshaft timing pinion and the bearing.

Cam wear, particularly on the exhaust lobes, had become a problem. To counter this, drillings in the timing-side crankcase now carried oil under pressure into the barrel casting and thence to both exhaust cam lobes. A modified timing cover was part of the revised system, and, from engine number DU 42399, a dowel was introduced between the crankcase and cylinder base to stop oil pressure loss should there be a gasket leakage.

The previously optional high-performance, 1⅛in-radius cam followers now became standard, with E4819 inlet and E4855 exhaust cams to suit.

Revised chromed pushrod tubes with flanged ends were sealed at top and bottom by square-section silicone rubber O-rings. So-called Red Spot inner and outer valve springs were introduced, as were higher-compression 9:1 pistons. From engine number DU 39464, the troublesome alloy exhaust stubs reverted to the steel type.

Graham Bowen's superbly restored UK-market T120 dates from 1968 – a year that was a high point in Bonneville production. Concentric carburettors supplanted Monoblocs during the 1967 season.

Otherwise, exhausts stayed as before, with the exception of the US T120C competition model, covered in the next chapter.

1967

Commencing with engine number DU 44394, the changes to the Bonneville for 1967 may not have been as numerous as the preceding year, but they were significant. Probably the most important was that Triumph was now fitting Hepolite pistons, which were complemented shortly afterwards – from engine number DU 47006 – by stronger con rods with an increased cross-section.

A new E3134-form exhaust cam was fitted to suit the high-performance inlet cam already in use. Efforts to reduce exhaust cam wear continued, initially with the introduction of a new metering dowel with a 'jiggle pin' incorporated in the feed jet to ensure it did not become blocked, allied to a gauze filter at the timing cover union where the

A far from immaculate, but authentic, 1969 US T120R re-imported from the 'States by ex-Meriden staffer Clive Humphries. Twin-leading-shoe brake was introduced for 1968. Lower trim on seat should be chrome and paintwork is faded, but otherwise this is a fine specimen.

feed was taken from. From engine number DU 63043, this was scrapped in favour of drillings in the tappet blocks, providing a timed feed to the cam via the cam followers themselves. As each exhaust cam's follower came off its base circle, a cut-out on its stem transferred oil from a port in the tappet block, which gained a sealing O-ring at its base after engine number DU 63241. Also new in the lubrication system was an oil pump with improved scavenge capacity.

Slight exhaust system changes saw the down-pipe cross-braces become two separate pieces that attached to the crankcase on either side. In the UK, the smaller US-pattern silencers became an increasingly popular option.

1968

Hepolite pistons were again specified, but now improved by extra metal in the crown and behind the ring lands. Green Spot outer valve springs

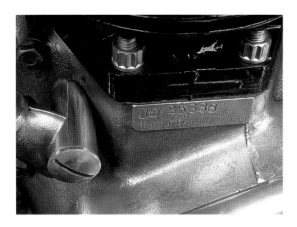

From 1969, engine numbers (far left) were displayed over a series of 'Triumph' trademark stampings to combat theft. This is a 1970 model with the 12-point cylinder base nuts adopted from 1968. Crankcase breather changes for 1970 include main vent (left) now exiting from rear of primary chaincase.

allowed higher valve lift while maintaining the same loading during closure. From engine number DU 79965, the oil feeds through the rocker arms to their rubbing faces were discontinued, strengthening the rocker arms. The cylinder block now had 12-point holding-down nuts, which made it easier to tighten the block evenly, using a suitable ring spanner. The exhaust system was largely unchanged, although US models were modified after engine number DU 75452 because of problems with baffles becoming detached. The access hole for the TDC timing tool moved, after engine number DU66246, from the upper face of the main casing behind the cylinder block to a location below the front engine mounting.

As the factory and service shops had been setting ignition at 38 degrees BTDC with the aid of a strobe lamp for some time, the crank flywheel now had two notches. One engaged at TDC and the other at 38 degrees BTDC. To make this practice easier, a new primary drive cover, with a round inspection cover (bearing a black Triumph logo) over the alternator, was introduced. After engine number DU 83021 the primary chaincase also carried a static timing mark, which could be aligned with the 38-degree mark on the rotor to assist those without access to a strobe light.

It was soon realised that the new position for the timing tool at the front of the crankcases was of more use as an oil drain plug, so the positioning boss for the tool returned to its previous position behind the cylinder block. After engine number DU 74052, the facility for the tool was only available at the original position behind the cylinder block. A change to the ignition contact breaker assembly meant a new points cover.

1969

If the T120 engine was good in 1968, it got better in 1969. The single most significant improvement was probably the nitride-hardened camshafts that ended premature wear once and for all. Nitrided replacement camshafts – easily identified by a capital N stamped on them – were made available for earlier machines.

The year's production began at engine number DU 85904. But starting with number DU 86965, Bonneville engine numbers were stamped over a series of stamped Triumph motifs, to make illicit changes more difficult. The number remained in its usual site on a raised pad just below the cylinder base joint on the left side.

More Unified threads were used in 1969 engines, including crankcase joints and all outer cover fasteners.

From engine number DU 85904, revised Hepolite pistons with domed crowns and gudgeon pins of increased section were specified. From engine number GC 23016, new conrods with self-locking cap nuts appeared. As a result of new thread forms, big-end bolt tightening torque was reduced from 28lb ft to 22. To reduce vibration, a heavier crankshaft flywheel – still with the 85 per cent balance factor – arrived at engine number NC 02256.

Pushrod tubes were revised to improve oil retention. The new type was castellated at the top, and sealed at both ends by Viton round-section O-rings. As this revision was not entirely successful, a further change was made at engine number PD 32574: an extra collar pressed over the tube's lower end retained a rubber washer around the base of the tappet block in a belt-and-braces attempt at preventing the escape of lubricant.

Further refinements included an increase in the size of the oil pump feed plunger, together with a scavenge pipe shortened at the sump end, raising the ambient oil level. The rev counter drive unit's mount switched to a left-hand (Unified) thread to prevent it from working loose.

The most obvious change to the exhaust system was the adoption of a balance pipe between the two downpipes, running horizontally across the front of the cylinder head close to the exhaust ports. This feature, seen on Thruxton T120 racers from 1965, reduced noise output while maintaining efficiency. It also meant that UK customers could now enjoy the more attractive short, sport silencers already standard in the USA. An electric oil pressure sensor was also provided on the timing cover, protected by a rubber sheath.

A 1970 US-market T120R in Astral Red and Silver. Mudguards on US models by this stage were painted in the main colour. Exhaust system's horizontal balance pipe, introduced in 1969, can be seen between the downpipes.

1970

There were a number of modifications for 1970, starting at engine number JD 24849, although the overall look and feel of the Bonneville motor was not greatly changed.

Crankcase ventilation was revised and the timed breather no longer fitted. Instead, a row of three small holes in the left-side crankcase half, just rearwards of the main bearing boss, vented into the primary chaincase. From there, an opening behind the clutch allowed excess pressure to escape via an elbow pipe that emerged from the primary case. The vent pipe was clipped to the left side of the rear mudguard, running to the rear of the machine. The new system had the benefit of providing a constant level of lubricant in the primary case, since oil could drain back into the engine if the level reached the three holes.

New camshafts with UNF threads for the gear-securing nuts were now housed in pre-sized bushes, while the timing gears were also new for 1970. These incorporated tapped holes to accept gear pullers for easy removal. Separate triangular front engine mounting plates made engine removal easier, but were primarily intended to facilitate assembly at Meriden, where T120 production sometimes neared 900 units a week.

The alternator cable was now re-routed over the top of the gearbox casing and the engine drive sprocket regained its spacer. The rev counter drive's body casting was modified to eliminate the pressed-in plug used formerly.

Fuel system & carburettors

1966

Larger 1⁵⁄₁₆in carburettors without lock-wiring on the float bowl covers were fitted after engine number DU 29738. From engine number DU 34086, they received a number 4 slide cutaway and the needle position was moved to number 2. Some US East Coast road models also gained separate round pancake air filters, improving accessibility to the ignition switch.

1967

The Bonneville started the year wearing the old Amal Type 389 Monobloc carburettors with 240 main jets. By engine number DU 59320, these had been usurped by new Concentric carburettors from Amal. Choke sizes were now quoted in millimetres rather than the old Imperial measurements and, for 1967, they were 30mm.

For the first time, the Bonneville was equipped with a cold-starting choke mechanism, controlled by a handlebar lever near the front brake lever. The new Concentric carburettor was slimmer in profile than the Monobloc and featured an integral float bowl with its float concentric with the centrally located main jet.

The pairs of Concentrics could be adjusted easily from either side and supposedly gave smoother carburation, but many riders believe the Monobloc is a better-quality item. Air filtration remained the preserve of the US models, although they did switch to the individual round type filters with felt elements.

1968

The 30mm Concentric carburettors remained, with minor internal changes to cure the slides of a tendency to stick. Air filters were still optional on UK machines at the start of the year, but became standard equipment later. For the US market the filter mountings were changed to a screw-on type which threaded directly on to the carburettor intakes.

1969

Although 30mm Concentric carburettors were again standard, they no longer had separate pilot jets, relying on a fixed internal drilling. Main jet size dropped from 210 to 190 and the needle jets from 0.107 to 0.106. The carburettors got partial rubber mounting for 1969 as well, with O-rings at the carburettor-to-flange faces and rubber washers under the mounting nuts.

1970

The only change here was the welcome addition of plastic plugs in the base of the Amal Type 930 carburettors' float bowls, permitting easy draining of fuel and residue.

Transmission

1966

Internal changes to the gearbox were confined to removal of the speedometer drive from the end of

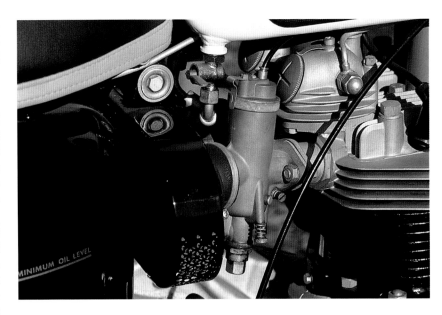

the layshaft and the drive cable's take-off from the gearbox inner cover. A longer kick-start lever was introduced to cope with the increased compression ratio.

Inside the primary chaincase, a new clutch adjusting screw appeared from engine number DU 31168 onwards. The metered oil feed to the final drive chain was blanked-off after engine number DU 27893, when a metered supply was provided from inside the oil tank's filler neck. A broader primary chain tensioner blade appeared after engine number DU 22590.

1967

Layshaft splines had their sharp edges relieved to reduce the risk of stress fractures, which had been reported under hard competition use in the USA. Also Loctite plastic gasket was used to prevent oil leakage past the gearbox sprocket. Between engine numbers DU 64758 and 64858, alternate engagement dogs were removed from the second gear pinion on the mainshaft.

By now, the factory was starting to implement a change in fastener thread forms, from British Standard fine and coarse (BSF and Whitworth) and Cycle Engineers Institute (CEI), to Unified fine and coarse (UNF and UNC). The gearbox of the 1967 Bonneville was one of the first items to feel the wind of this particular change.

From engine number DU 48114, the mainshaft was lengthened and a self-locking Unified nut and plain washer fitted to attach the clutch hub. After engine number DU 48145, all gearbox threads were changed to Unified forms.

1968

The mainshaft now featured UNF threads at both ends and a new mainshaft high gear with an extended nose, which butted up directly to the oil seal. The new arrangement required a new inner

This integral air filter, serving both carburettors, was replaced during the 1966 season by individual pancake filters. Stained carburettors indicate that this immaculate US T120R is used.

cover plate to the primary drive case as well. A revised camplate plunger and holder improved the gearchange, while, on the outside of the 'box, the gearchange lever rubber became a dumbbell-shaped moulding also seen on BSA products. The kick-start mechanism gained Unified threads, as did the new clutch shock absorber spider, which also required a UNF threaded extractor.

1969

Most of the gearbox internals changed in 1969. From engine number DU 88630, a new camplate appeared, followed at JD 26313 by a new gearchange quadrant. Third gear ratio was amended from 22/24 to 22/23. All gear pinions underwent a new hardening treatment and an extra machining process on their teeth to reduce both wear and noise – these are known as 'shaved' gears. From engine number CC 15546, mainshaft and layshaft diameters and pinion internal diameters were increased, completing almost total revision of the gearbox. A statically balanced clutch basket from engine number DU 88383 was the only other transmission update for the year.

1970

The gearbox now came in for extensive revision. Modification of the inner cover allowed the use of a shorter selector rod and a more substantial mainshaft bearing circlip after engine number AD 37473. Aluminium-bronze selector forks incorporating rollers replaced steel forks after engine number ED 51080, and a precision-pressed camplate and leaf spring appeared at engine number ED 52044. The only downside of these gearbox developments was that they combined to make stripping the 'box a much trickier and more time-consuming affair.

Stainless steel mudguards were fitted front and rear to US models in 1966. Polished alloy rear light housing was new that year too.

Frame & rear suspension
1966

A number of modifications were made to the frame. To improve high-speed handling, a new cast steering head lug, which altered the steering angle to 62 degrees, was used from engine number DU 25277. Fairing mounts had been added to the front of the steering stem, and, at this point, Unified thread forms were beginning to replace the British Standard threads traditionally used at Meriden. UNF (fine) threads appeared on several fasteners relating to the front frame section.

The new 12-volt electrics involved the battery carrier being modified to carry a pair of batteries. Round pegs were incorporated onto the rear subframe to take a new carrier frame, secured to the pegs by rubber-bushed tubular ends on a retaining strap. Threaded bars on the battery carrier provided a mounting for the revised left-side panel housing the ignition and light switches. A slightly larger tool tray was moulded in plastic.

Rear suspension units remained unchanged, but the swinging arm was widened by having its right-side leg moved out by ¼in to accommodate tyres of wider selection.

1967

Frame changes were minimal in 1967. At the front, threaded adjustable lock-stops were provided to exploit the greater lock afforded by slimmer fuel tanks. For the first time, the Bonneville gained a proper steering security lock and an extension on the left of the steering head casting provided a socket for the lock to slide into. Some of the rear subframe fasteners changed to the Unified thread type.

1968

Modifications to the frame for 1968 were relatively minor, although between engine numbers DU75430 and DU 75449 heavier-gauge tube was tried for the manufacture of the front frame. At the front, the steering lock socket on the steering head casting was lengthened and the propstand lug was revised, along with the stand itself which lost its 'foot' in favour of a curved end which made it easier to operate.

At the rear, a new swinging arm lug was introduced and, from engine number DU 81196, a new swinging arm of heavier (12swg) tubing appeared. Its beefier gusseting stiffened up the rear end of the machine considerably.

The rear subframe was altered to accommodate the new mounting arrangements for the left side panel, which now doubled as a tool box. No longer carrying switches, the panel was attached by means of rubber bushed pegs welded to the subframe at the rear, while at the top front of the panel a plastic threaded knob secured the panel precariously to the frame. After repeated reports of the knob vibrating off in use, a spring clip was used, with only marginal success, to retain the knob on its thread.

1969

The frame itself received no modification for 1969, but a couple of tweaks were made to the rear suspension. The swinging arm, although visually identical to the previous type, was of still heavier-gauge tubing, while the Girling shock absorbers lost their black-enamelled shrouds so that their chromed springs were openly displayed.

1970

Changes to the frame were limited to the new separate front engine mounting plates and the fitting of an adjustable stop for the prop stand to protect the exhaust pipe. The Girling rear suspension units gained castellated pre-load adjuster sleeves designed to prevent ingress of road dirt and grit.

Steering & front suspension

1966

The only fork change for 1966 was a modified lower yoke, fitted from engine number DU 27672 to provide increased steering lock, made possible by that year's fuel tank change. At DU 31119, a plastic steering damper sleeve replaced the alloy item. Early machines featured 'white' (actually very pale grey) handlebar grips, but later in the year more practical black versions appeared.

1967

A new top yoke carried the Yale-type barrel steering lock, while an O-ring groove was machined into the dust excluder sleeve nuts. Further down the fork, black wire spring-clips replaced the worm-drive Jubilee clips that held the fork gaiters. On the handlebars, thicker soft plastic Grand Turismo grips were fitted.

1968

New forks were fitted for 1968, although they looked virtually identical to the units they replaced. The main difference was the two-way shuttle valve damping, a great improvement over the old set-up. From engine number DU 68363, the fork assembly joined the move to Unified threads, while at the top of the new forks the left-hand combined fork shroud and headlamp bracket now carried the ignition switch.

1969

New fork yokes, with stanchion centres now ¼in wider apart at 6¾in, allowed the fitting of larger-section front tyres and, from engine number AC

10464, two extra drillings in the stanchions considerably improved rebound damping characteristics. A longer front wheel spindle was necessary, as was an extended brakeplate location lug on the right-side fork slider. A chromed steering stem top nut took the place of the traditional steering damper that was now only supplied to special order, and rubber ties now secured electrical cables neatly to the 'bars.

1970

The looks of the fork assembly were not significantly changed, but from engine number AC 10464 there were new pressed steel mudguard mounting plates on the sliders and, internally, two additional bleed holes in each stanchion.

Precision-ground hard chromium plate now applied to the outer surfaces of the stanchions was a major improvement. Handlebar control pivots now carried provision for the fitting of mirrors at their bases, and chromed steel clips restrained the dipswitch wiring.

Wheels, brakes & tyres

1966

Tyre sizes were unchanged for 1966, but the front brake drum gained a massive 46 per cent increase in friction area. This was achieved by moving the right-side spokes out onto a raised flange on the wheel hub, allowing wider brake shoes to be used. At the rear, both the standard and QD versions of the wheel were modified to accept the speedometer drive, which was now better placed to deal with changes of overall gearing. The standard rear hub now had a bolted-on 46-tooth sprocket replacing the previous integral type.

1967

On UK and general export machines, a 19in front

Original, but old and cracked. 'White' handlebar grips were fitted for 1966 only.

Flanged front hub (above left) was introduced for 1966. A 1968 front wheel (above right) shows the twin-leading-shoe brake – Triumph's best-ever drum – introduced that year; cable and operating arms were later to be revised.

Rear brake rod arrangement and brake light switch seen on a 1968 UK-market T120.

US-market 1966 T120R in Alaskan White and Grenadier Red. Altered rev counter drive from exhaust camshaft gives better cable run to the revised instrument head.

Block-lettered Bonneville transfer on side panel and simplified tank badge were new for 1969. Passenger grab rail bolts to underside of seat.

All-chrome grab rail indicates that this US T120R is from late 1970. Early versions for that year had the rail finished in black and chrome.

wheel rim was specified, replacing the 18in version. The Dunlop ribbed pattern tyre was a 3.00 x 19in on these models. In the US, wheels and tyres were unchanged, although the optional 4.00 x 18in size was gaining increasing favour on off-road models.

1968

The principal and most welcome change of 1968 was the twin-leading-shoe front brake fitted to all T120s. The existing 8in full-width cast-iron hub was modified to accept the larger TLS brake plate. With its extended and polished perimeter, the new brake plate looked impressive and was effective too. Each brake shoe was lifted by its own operating cam, doubling the self-servo effect by having two leading edges against the drum instead of one. An adjustable rod linked the external operating levers, ensuring that the cams worked together. The cast alloy backplate featured a mesh-covered air scoop at the front and an exit vent at the rear.

The operating cable outer butted against an anchor point cast onto the backplate, and, from engine number DU 70083, this was drilled and fitted with a pin to prevent the cable outer jumping out of its socket in the event of it being too slack. The only problem with the new set-up was the length of the cable and the tortuous route it was forced to take. Passing behind the head-lamp, the cable was clipped to the bottom yoke before passing through a rectangular retaining loop on the mudguard and being tied on to the rear of the mudguard stay on its way to the brake plate. In practice, the cable could get trapped under the rear edge of the mudguard when the forks compressed. Action at the hand lever also tended to be spongy.

A longer mudguard fitted during the year cured the trapping problem, but it would take a redesigned brake operating linkage the following year to eliminate the sponginess.

On the other side of the front hub, a new chromed dust cover with ten louvres around its periphery was attached by three screws.

The rear wheel was unchanged for 1968, the only other update being a tyre change for some US machines, which gained 3.25 x 19in Dunlop K70 front tyres to match the rear.

1969

Revision to the front brake did away with the excessive cable run and its associated sponginess of operation. This was achieved by re-siting the cable location on the backplate and providing the operating arm with a straight lever for the cable to pull upwards on. The two operating arms were still linked, but now via a cranked lever at the front, at an angle to the actual operating arm. This new arrangement meant that a shorter cable run – straight up the back of the right fork leg – could be used, giving a much more positive feel. At last, the Bonneville had the front brake it deserved.

On the other side of the wheel, a plainer, pressed-on hub trim with concentric rings replaced the cheap and nasty-looking louvred trim.

1970

A flat-section rear brake torque arm replaced the previous tubular item, and the rear wheel received UNF fasteners in line with the gradual overall conversion.

Seat & bodywork

1966

The seat cover remained as the familiar two-tone grey and black version in the UK, but some US road machines and most of the off-roaders wore plain black.

Mudguard specifications varied greatly during 1966. UK models retained painted steel guards, finished in Alaskan White with a Grenadier Red centre stripe and gold pinstriping. In the US, road models wore polished stainless steel guards with rolled side edges, and the front mudguard's rear stay, previously doubling as a front stand, was replaced by a simple tubular loop stay which was enamelled black. Off-road machines for the US West Coast had alloy mudguards.

Petrol tanks were all changed in 1966. For the UK market, the tank capacity remained at 4 gallons, although the tank itself was an all-new welded steel affair with a slimmer profile, as seen from the top. The parcel rack was still specified in the UK and the tank still carried a chromed centre strip and glued on knee-grips. In the 'States, the new tank was much smaller, at 2½ US gallons, and assumed the attractive teardrop shape that was to become synonymous with US Bonnevilles. Known as the 'slimline' in America, the tank's sleek shape did much to boost sales. At long last, the Bonneville shed the tank-top rack – in the

'States at least – that was so out of tune with the machine's sporting image. Knee-grips remained, although American models now had the thinner glued-on versions.

For all markets, 1966 tanks wore new badges. It was 'goodbye' to the 'harmonica' grille used by Triumph since 1957 and 'hello' to a new shape of chrome-plated emblem sometimes called the 'eyebrow' badge. The Triumph name was in black on a white ground.

UK models were finished in Grenadier Red over Alaskan White with a gold separating line. In the US, the slimline tanks were finished in all-over Alaskan White with a broad centre stripe in Grenadier Red, flanked by two thinner stripes of the same colour. The effect of this scheme of racy orange – the true hue of Grenadier Red – against white was stunning.

A new 6-pint oil tank gained the metering device in its neck already described. The new design allowed the oil tank transfers to return to their former position, out of sight under the seat. Finish on both the oil tank and the corresponding switch panel on the left of the machine was all-black, as was the chainguard. The only other significant change in pressed-steel ware for the year was the adoption on US machines of a simple strip mounting for the rear licence plate in place of the large black number plate which continued on UK models.

1967

After being unchanged for many years, the seat assembly was replaced by a new type, narrower at the nose to complement the slimline fuel tank. A slight step halfway along its top meant pillion passengers sat slightly higher and helped keep the rider firmly anchored under hard acceleration. The new seat top may have helped in this respect too, as it featured quilted crossways ribs along its entire length. Finish was two-tone at first, with a grey top separated from the black sides by white piping, with a grey trim around the bottom. At the back, a gold Triumph logo appeared across the rear of the seat. The plan was to use this scheme for T120R models and to use all-black seats for the off-road T120C, but most US machines, on-road or off-road, ended up with all black seats as the year progressed, although UK models mainly got the grey top finish.

Fuel tanks remained the same for 1967, apart from finish, although the mounting studs were converted to UNF threads. Colours for the home market were Aubergine and Alaskan White, but the division between the colours changed slightly. The lower colour now extended to the rear of the tank and over the top of the rubber knee grips. At the front, the lower colour now extended upwards, covering all of the front of the tank,

Introduced for the 'States in 1966, slimline fuel tank holds 2½ US gallons and has glued-on knee-grips.

before curving rearwards to finish in a 'V' alongside the filler cap. Once again a gold line separated the two colours.

In the US, things were more complicated. The market demanded more lively colours and early 1967 models were finished in Aubergine over Gold, separated by a white line. At first, the colour separation was the same as in the UK, but later some models featured a top colour that curved back inboard at the rear of the knee grips, finishing under the front of the seat. Problems arose when dealers discovered the Gold lower colour was sensitive to sunlight and fading while still in showrooms, so, after engine number DU 48157, the lower colour was changed to Alaskan White, as on home-market machines.

Mudguards were another example of growing variations between the home and US markets. For the UK, the mild steel guards were finished in Aubergine, with an Alaskan White centre stripe and gold pinstriping. US models continued with stainless steel and rolled side edges. The oil tank was unchanged, while the left side panel now only carried the ignition switch and its front mounting was welded rather than screwed in place. Both continued to be finished in black.

1968

The seat gained extra padding, along with new folding hinges. Finish on UK models remained two-tone as before, but with a chromed plastic trim strip on the lower edge. US-market seats were now black with black plastic trim. From engine number DU75452, the seat strap fitted to US West Coast machines was replaced by a chromed grab rail at the rear of the seat. East Coast versions acquired the rail from engine number DU 77018.

Mudguards for all models now featured rolled leading and trailing edges to complement their rolled sides. As mentioned earlier, the front guard was lengthened on home-market models from engine number DU 81709, but US riders had to take their chances with trapped front brake cables. US guards remained polished stainless steel and the UK models were painted Silver with a Hi-Fi Scarlet stripe lined in gold.

Slimline US tanks were unchanged except for colour, which was solid Hi-Fi Scarlet with a Silver centre stripe with gold lining. A gold 'Bonneville' transfer was applied diagonally, opposite the tank filler, while the 'Made in England' transfer disappeared completely from the tank. In the UK, the fuel tank finish followed the same pattern as the previous year, with the top colour being Hi-Fi Scarlet and the lower (but increasingly dominant) colour Silver. A smaller knee-grip rubber and new fuel tap washers incorporating rubber O-rings after engine number DU 77670 were the only other changes to the fuel tank.

The oil tank now featured the rocker feed take-off in its integral return line and was again finished in black. A new, larger gold Bonneville transfer on the side of the now switch-less left side panel could actually be read from further away than three inches! At the front end, the black left-side headlamp bracket was the new home for the 'World Speed Record Holder' transfer. To comply with highway regulations, American models also acquired round amber side reflectors housed in sheet metal covers affixed to the fuel tank mounts.

1969

Changes to the seat were minor. The quilted top of the cover was now of aerated material and UK models gained the threaded holes in the base to attach a rear grab rail, which the US market machines had received in 1968. At the same time, UK models came into line with their American counterparts by wearing the same all-black finish on their dual seats.

On the Bonneville's fuel tank, the 'eyebrow' badge reached the end of its brief run, replaced by a smaller, simpler emblem. Still chrome-backed, this badge lacked the 'wing' on its leading edge.

Colours for 1969 were Olympic Flame (a deep orangey-red) over Silver. UK models retained the previous year's fuel tank, but in the USA it was all-change again. Early in the season, the US tank was as in 1968, but later a thin flash of Silver curled rearwards from the top front of the tank badge, ending in a point towards the back of the tank, on either side of its centre seam.

Still later, the most common US colour scheme for the year included an extra lower flash of Silver. This started from the base of the new tank badge and extended downwards and rearwards before ending in a point under the front of

The 1968 seat featured a grey quilted top with thicker padding and external hinges attached to the seat base.

Chrome grab rail and 'aerated' seat cover, seen on US T120R, were both new for 1970.

the knee-grip rubber. In all cases, white pinstriping separated the main colours.

Mudguards remained painted steel in both the UK and the USA, and were finished in Silver with an Olympic Flame centre stripe with gold pinstriping in the UK and white for the USA. A few US machines had the mudguard colours reversed, but it is not known how many, or indeed why.

The oil tank and left side panel remained unaltered for 1969, but the transfers on both oil and fuel tanks were new. Gone was the flowing script of the previous year, replaced by more modern block capitals. A small version of the new 'Bonneville' transfer took the usual position on the fuel tank opposite the filler, while the left panel received a larger version.

US machines kept the sticker on the right side of the machine just below the steering head, declaring the date and place of origin together with the fact that the machine complied with relevant safety regulations, as required by the US Department of Transportation. At the front of the machine, a hole in the right-hand headlamp bracket, suitably lined with a rubber grommet, allowed the throttle cables to pass through.

1970
A welded-on grab rail introduced on the rear mudguard mounting loop meant that the seat base lost the threaded holes for the previous grab rail. The seat was lowered by slight modification of the pan, and the rear guard was also drilled to allow the D-section breather from the primary case to be clipped to its left side. Colours for both guards were Astral Red (a kind of metallic maroon) with a silver centre stripe with gold pinstriping, the stripes finishing short of the rolled leading and trailing edges of the guards.

For all markets, Bonneville mudguard stays were chromed for 1970, and the front ones were modified to attach to the new mounting brackets on the fork sliders. The top and front stays now bolted through the new bracket into captive nuts held in a channel at the rear.

Fuel tanks were the same as before apart from the new season's colours. UK machines had a fresh look, being in Astral Red with a side panel of Silver, while US models wore the final 1969 colour layout; transfers were unchanged. A new 5½-pint oil tank was finished in black to match the side panel on the opposite side.

Electrics
1966
The introduction of 12-volt electrics was a significant change for 1966. The new 12-volt alternator involved a change to Lucas MA12 ignition coils, which remained in their usual hiding place under the tank. Apart from the new ignition switch (with its proper Yale-type key) and cut-out button, the ignition system remained as before.

As part of the new system, a Zener diode was incorporated to control charging of the paired Lucas MKZ9E six-volt batteries on early models and a single PUZ5A from engine number DU 32994. The rectifier got an improved bracket from engine number DU 27007 and the chromed headlamp shell housed green ignition and red main-beam warning lamps from engine number DU 31565. After engine number DU 32898, the Zener diode's heat sink was changed to a new right-angled type. From engine number DU 30800, the earthing tag was relocated from between the diode and its mounting and fitted to the rear of the heat sink.

US models received a new rear light, housed in a polished alloy casting, and also a large ignition cut-out button on the right of the handlebar. Different cut-outs were used, depending on the ignition system. A type with a black centre button was used on the off-roader's AC ignition, while the DC system's cut-out had a brown button.

1967
The only change to the ignition system was the adoption of a new auto-advance unit to counteract random spark problems that had appeared since the change to 12-volt electrics.

The main electrical change occurred at engine number DU58565, the introduction of resin-encapsulated alternator stator windings putting an end to premature vibration-induced failure. Other changes were the re-siting of the lighting switch to the rear of the headlamp shell and the use of a louder Lucas 6H horn. After engine DU59230, Mazda bulbs replaced Lucas items.

1968

Changes to the timing marks and the use of the timing tool have been described in the engine section. Apart from the new ease of locating 38 degrees BTDC, the new points set-up was the most significant revision in this area. The Lucas 6CA contact breaker assembly fitted for 1968 had two independently mounted and adjustable pairs of contact breakers, each on their own separate backing plate. This meant that the ignition timing could be set precisely for each cylinder. Felt lubrication pads were added to reduce wear on the nylon heels of the contact breakers from engine number DU 82146. A deeper points cover was also needed. The new assembly featured UNF fasteners and, because space in the new points compartment was limited, the twin capacitors were relocated under the fuel tank's front mounting.

The Zener diode was switched to a more sensible location under the bottom fork yoke, to receive cool air flow. It now also resided under a plastic bung in a heavily finned, dome-shaped, cast alloy heat sink. US models had yet another rear light and housing, now with red reflectors on its sides. UK machines adopted a new rear number plate which was wider at the top, where it featured two fixing points.

1969

The most obvious change was the adoption of twin 'windtone' horns, and from engine number CC 14783 these were replaced by even louder versions. These domed units, with relays to protect wiring and switchgear from the increased current they drew, hung below the front of the fuel tank, in the case of US machines from strengthened side-reflector supports, which UK versions lacked.

Just as important, although not as obvious, was the change to a higher-output Lucas RM21 encapsulated alternator stator. UK Bonnevilles were supplied with US-pattern rear stop and tail lights, a fitting made possible by the new rear number plate used on home-market machines. Further additions to the electrical system were the introduction of a front brake light switch in the brake cable and an oil pressure warning lamp that was only illuminated, like the ignition warning lamp, if there was trouble when the engine was running.

1970

The only change to ignition and timing was the adoption of smaller oil-filled Lucas 17M 12 coils.

New, larger pairs of windtone horns appeared for 1970 and their mountings sported extra sliding brackets from engine number ED 44339 to prevent them fouling the front mudguard when the forks were fully compressed. Headlamp bulb holders changed, causing a change of part number for the headlamp.

View under the tank of 1968 UK T120 shows cutaway area housing ignition coils. Horn bracket can also be seen.

Ignition switch moved from the front of the left side panel to a more sensible location on the left headlamp bracket for 1968.

Correct black-painted aluminium ties attach electrical cables to frame.

Twin Windtone horns
and strengthened
mounting brackets on
1970 US model, with
orange side reflectors
to comply with safety
regulations.

Grey-faced Smiths
clocks with 150mph
speedometer, first
seen in 1967.

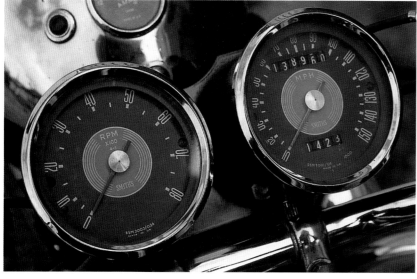

Instruments

1966

The speedometer head was unchanged, but drive from the rear wheel obviously entailed a longer cable. The tachometer was new, a change made necessary by the use of a 2:1 right-angle drive gearbox from the drive-side end of the exhaust cam, easing the cable's route considerably.

1967

A new 150mph Smiths magnetic speedometer was specified for 1967. The tachometer drive gearbox now featured a sealing washer, both to prevent leaks and reduce the incidence of the unit working loose in service.

1968

The new 7in headlamp shell now played host to a three-position lighting switch and a silicone-damped ammeter. As in the previous year, the ignition switch was in the left headlamp bracket.

1969

There were no changes to instruments for 1969.

1970

At the start of the year the instruments remained unchanged, but, later in the season, clocks with black-faced dials replaced the grey-faced instruments previously employed.

THE 750 T120RT BONNEVILLE FOR AMERICA

In America, the demands of competition riders had long been influential in the development of the Bonneville. When the American Motorcyclist Association (AMA) upped the capacity limit for ohv engines in dirt racing to 750cc in 1969, the call went out for a fully competitive big-bore version of the twin. AMA homologation rules demanded that at least 200 machines, or the tuning parts to convert a standard model, were made available for sale, but the factory was not willing to produce a 750cc version of the Bonneville for such a limited clientele.

The answer, as often before, came from the ingenuity and skills of the American importers. They looked to drag racer and accessory maker Hubert 'Sonny' Routt, who marketed Webcor big-bore kits for boosting the 650 Triumph's capacity, one of them raising it to near 750cc.

Tricor (Triumph's East Coast operation) realised that this was a rapid route to homologation and ordered more than 200 kits, specially finished to look like a Meriden product externally. Kits were duly supplied, consisting of new iron barrels, pistons, rings, circlips, gudgeon pins, head and base gaskets, tappet feed plug and centre head bolt with washer. The forged pistons were 0.008in oversize to fit Routt's 3in cylinder bores.

Tricor assembled 145 T120RT models, while Triumph's West Coast HQ in Duarte, California, built another 55. The conversions were fitted to standard machines before they were uncrated and for that reason only the engine numbers had the T suffix stamped after the Meriden number. Only that and small cast-in MC (Motor Castings, Routt's chosen foundry) trademarks on the base of the block near the tappet blocks gave the game away. The only other difference from the standard T120R was the instruction issued to dealers to fit 376/100-200 main jets in the carburettors as a safety measure. The AMA approved the T120RT, but it would be more than two years before a genuine Meriden-built 750cc Bonneville appeared.

Chapter 6

Competition variants:1960-70 TR7B, T120C and TT Special

Given that the Bonneville was always intended as a high-performance machine, it is not surprising that the factory should have produced pure competition variants. It may seem odd that it took so long after the model's inception, but factory racing projects were viewed with disapproval under Edward Turner's reign.

For the US market, however, it was essential for Triumph to continue a tradition of supplying machines in suitable trim for TT Scrambles, desert racing, enduros and other forms of competition. The street-equipped Bonneville Scrambler was offered from 1960, at first coded TR7B, then T120C from 1961 to 1965.

TT Special

In 1963, US West Coast Triumph distributors Johnson Motors were responsible for the birth of the pure competition TT Special. Intended for

First of the TT Specials built expressly for competition – the 1963 T120C.

desert and dirt track racing, the Special took its name from TT dirt events, which incorporated jumps and both left and right turns.

How successful the Triumph was in its specific environment can be gauged from the fact that it won its first competitive outing, in the hands of Skip Van Leeuwen at the Ascot Park TT track in Southern California.

TT Specials were also used for drag racing or registered for road use, and the model could claim to be the fastest standard motorcycle of its day: *Cycle World* magazine squeezed 123.5mph out of its 1963 test machine.

Coded T120C, frames and most cycle parts are the same as the rest of the range for any given year, as it was mostly in the engine and exhaust systems that TT Specials stood apart. Accordingly, only significant differences between the T120R and C models and the TT Specials will be detailed. First catalogued for 1963, the TT Specials were listed until 1967 during which time some 3500 were believed to have been produced. Buyers today

should be aware that some stock T120s have become TT Specials during restoration.

1963

Larger 1³⁄₁₆in Amal Monobloc carburettors and gorgeous high-level chrome exhausts were the most striking visual features of the TT. The exhaust pipes were, in fact, the same as fitted to the T120C Bonnevilles with the substitution of straight-through end-pipes for the silencers supplied on the street scrambler. Engine numbers carried a T120C prefix like the street versions, giving rise to problems in identifying particular machines. Small oval heat shields protected the rider's leg – to a certain extent. There were no lights but otherwise changes that set the Special apart were hidden.

Quoted compression ratio was 12:1, but in reality 11.2:1 pistons were used. Together with the larger carburettors with 330 main jets, this boosted claimed power output by 2bhp to 52bhp. Inlet and exhaust cams were the same as in road-

Tank top rack and centre stand of this 1963 T120C have been removed, as was normal practice.

going models, but the TT Special's ignition system was an AC energy transfer system powered from the alternator. Early models came without air filtration, but later in the year a box-type filter serving both carburettors was introduced across the Bonneville range.

Cycle parts were only slightly changed from the road Bonnevilles. Petrol tanks were the TR6 Trophy type, finished in white and still with a chromed parcel rack. Sensible off-roaders removed it and filled the mounting holes with black rubber bungs available for the purpose.

Wheel rim sizes were 19in front and 18in rear, and TTs were usually shipped shod with Dunlop Trials Universal tyres of 3.50 x 19in and 4.00 x 18in sizes. These would often be changed according to proposed use. The dual seat was covered in two-tone grey and black vinyl (with grey on top). An alloy front mudguard was fitted, while the rear one was in white-painted steel with a raised central rib. Non-folding footrests were mounted on the rear engine plates and a sump guard (a TR6 item) was optional. No speedometer was fitted and the rev counter was carried in a special bracket mounted centrally on the upper fork yoke.

US-type handlebars perfectly complemented the lean, spare look of the new off-roader.

1964
A new cylinder head to suit larger mountings for Amal 1¹⁄₁₆in carburettors was fitted, and heat insulating blocks were provided between carburettors and head. Otherwise the engine was unchanged except for the reduction of the gearbox sprocket by one tooth to 18 teeth, requiring a shorter drive chain to be specified.

TT Specials benefited from the new front fork fitted across the range for 1964, but with top shrouds minus headlamp brackets and a TR6-type top yoke with integral handlebar clamps and a friction steering damper. A large ignition cut-out switch appeared on the right-hand handlebar and a new rev counter bracket placed the new Smiths magnetic instrument on the right of the top yoke.

Seats had all-black covers for 1964 and TR6 rear shock absorbers replaced Bonneville items. Both front and rear mudguards were alloy and the front guard got a new lower stay that replaced the front wheel stand type used in 1963. Fuel tank colours changed to Gold and White, in line with

Superb 1966 T120C with slimline fuel tank new for that year. No parcel rack, and with low-level TT pipes as had appeared the previous season.

Polished alloy mudguards indicate a West Coast model (above). This was the final year for pale handlebar grips. Although two-tone seats (below) appear in factory pictures of 1966 competition T120Cs, plain black covers were usual on competition machines.

road models. The specified tyres were now K70 Dunlop Gold Seals suitable for highway use, in the same sizes as before.

1965

Engine changes were confined to the slight reduction of compression ratio to 11:1 by the fitting of new pistons and rings. A batch of East Coast TT Specials (from engine number DU18838 to DU18880) was supplied with camshafts treated by the Tuftriding hardening process.

The main visual change was the introduction of the short, low-level exhaust system. Finishing level with the swinging arm spindle underneath the frame's lower rails, the new system was ideal for the TT and extremely popular. This exhaust spelled the end for the centre stand because of its postion. It was attached at the front by flat strips running between the front of the engine and welded-on threaded bosses at the downpipes, and at the rear by circular clamps.

Folding footrests appeared on the TTs, but the parcel rack remained. Some East Coast versions were supplied with painted alloy front mudguards and the old ribbed steel rear guards, but most TT

Colour scheme for 1966 was Alaskan White with Grenadier Red central striping on the fuel tank (left) – a particularly striking combination.

Specials persevered with polished alloy guards front and rear. The colour scheme for 1965 was Pacific Blue and Silver as on the road models, the mudguards being in silver with a blue centre stripe lined in gold. The new roadster fork also appeared on the TT Specials.

1966

This was the first year that engine numbers of TT Specials included the TT prefix. Early machines retained the T120C prefix, though, and it was to be later in the model year before the TT stamping featured. Engine modifications were limited to new camshafts but, at engine number DU31119, the exhaust cam was further updated. Carburettor float bowls lost their lockwire in 1966 and some East Coast models acquired larger individual air filters too. The gearbox sprocket lost yet another tooth, settling for 17 teeth, and the rear wheel sprocket now had 46 teeth.

On the chassis, the new slimline petrol tank with thinner glued-on rubber knee-grips meant no more luggage racks. Colours for 1966 were Alaskan White with two thin stripes in Grenadier Red flanking a thicker central one along the top of the tank.

A new ignition cut-out button was placed on the right of the handlebar and a number of machines wore the light grey Amal handlebar grips before black grips returned. The rev counter stayed where it was but a new Smiths instrument supplanted its predecessor. Mudguards again varied according to region, with the West Coast

Handlebar detail shows cut-out button and pale handgrip. A special bracket holds the lone instrument, a Smiths 10,000rpm tachometer.

The slimmed tank introduced in 1966 has directly glued-on knee-pads.

machines having alloy guards and some East Coast variants receiving steel guards painted in Alaskan White with Grenadier Red stripes lined in gold.

1967

The TT Specials mirrored the alterations to the rest of the Bonneville range. Engine changes were as for road models, although there were a few changes to cycle parts that were specific to the TT models. East and West Coast models finally fell into line with regard to mudguards, all TT models now being supplied with stainless steel mudguards front and rear.

Fuel tank colour was Aubergine with a Gold lower styling flash running down and back from the underside of the 'eyebrow' tank badge and underneath the rubber knee-grip. After engine number DU48157, this lower panel changed to Alaskan White. Seats were again black.

As it turned out, 1967 was the last year of production for the TT Special. It had been planned to produce the model for 1968 and, indeed, some transfers were actually produced for that year's intended production. But in the event the TT Special bowed out of Meriden's US catalogue.

T120 Thruxton Bonneville

In Britain, the notion of a sporting Bonneville was light years away from the US desert racing and dirt track concept. In Europe the letters TT meant the Isle of Man Tourist Trophy road races: a competition Bonneville would have to show its mettle, if not on the legendary TT Mountain circuit, then at least on the UK's short circuits where potential buyers of Triumph's big twins flocked every weekend in the 1960s. The factory soon rose to the challenge, supplying works-prepared Bonnevilles to dealer entrants for major production class events. So the Thruxton Bonneville was born.

Named after the Hampshire circuit that usually hosted the year's most prestigious 500-mile production roadster race, the Thruxton Bonneville is a real rarity and can be difficult to define.

Machines in 'Thruxton trim' had been prepared for the 500-miler even in Tiger 110 days, when Mike Hailwood and Dan Shorey won the 1958 marathon on that model. It was the practice at that time to enter factory-prepared machines through dealers, as works entries were barred by the Production Class rules. Two small batches of 'Thruxtonised' T120s were assembled in 1964.

But at that year's Blackpool Show, the model name was applied officially for the first time to a bike on display, heralding a special version of the T120 to be built in a limited numbers for sale to the public, mainly to satisfy homologation rules. The batch assembled in May 1965 was intended to be 50 machines, but when the cylinder head

and carburettors from one (engine number DU 23156) were apparently stolen on the production line, the rest of that machine was broken for spares, leaving 49 examples.

The engine of the catalogued Thruxton featured a number of modifications. The most significant upgrade was the use of touring-profile E4220 camshafts, with larger (3in) radius cam followers to achieve a higher lift and greater duration of valve opening. The Thruxton also pioneered positive oil feed to the exhaust cam, which was to become standard on all Bonnevilles for the following year. In 1965 the feed was via an external small-bore pipe from the timing chest to the front of the cylinder block.

Transmissions were standard, although some Thruxtons were supplied with close-ratio gear clusters in standard gearbox cases. All Thruxtons benefited from careful assembly of selected and matched components.

Carburettors were 'chopped' Amal Monoblocs with a centrally mounted remote float chamber, though choke sizes remained the same as the roadster's at 1⅛in. A new exhaust system allowed the engine to produce enhanced power while running quietly enough to satisfy Production rules. Swept-back 1½in downpipes were linked by a balance pipe to increase the system's volume for each cylinder, and they narrowed to 1¼in below the balancer tube to promote higher gas speed.

Special, long 'straight-through' silencers were angled upwards at the rear for clearance and attached to the frame's seat loop by long, flat straps fixed to lugs on the silencers. Because the downpipes were tucked in and swept back, a detachable mid-section of the pipe had to be incorporated to give access to the primary drive cover and the timing chest. The factory reckoned a Thruxton gave 54bhp as opposed to the 47bhp claimed for the standard Bonneville.

The cycle parts gave the Thruxton its distinctive look. A little more cornering clearance was gained by using 19in wheels front and rear. Steepening the steering head angle, together with a revised head lug casting, significantly improved handling, and this alteration found its way on to the stock Bonneville for 1966. The Thuruxton's fork was upgraded, too, with shuttle valves to control damping, an improvement that reached the T120 roadster in 1968.

The 8in front brake, as fitted to the standard 1965 Bonneville, gained a forward-facing cooling air scoop on the Thruxton, but chromed steel wheel rims were retained. The chromed tank badges made way for simple transfers to save a few ounces. While the show machine had sported a parcel grid, production Thruxtons went without, having the mount holes plugged with US-market bungs. Handlebars had to use standard mountings

Magnificent 1968 road racer restored by Thruxton Bonneville specialist George Hopwood for owner Tony Sumner. This machine was originally supplied to Midlands dealer A. Bennett & Son, and raced in Production events by Daryl Pendlebury. On 1968-built racers, Thruxton exhaust pipes are routed high for maximum cornering clearance.

Fairing is an Avon brand item by Mitchenall Bros, who supplied a less sleek moulding for the earlier 1965 Thruxton. Handlebars are clip-on types; earlier UK Production rules had dictated that 'bars must use the standard mounts on the top yoke.

Seeley double-sided front brake was among special parts homologated for production racing, but not necessarily obtainable from Triumph dealers.

on the top yoke to comply with race regulations, leading to the adoption of downswept, M-shaped 'Thruxton bend' 'bars. An Avon AR Sport moulded fairing was added and Thruxton colours were the same Pacific Blue and Silver as the 1965 UK road models.

Behind the tank, a single racing saddle replaced the standard seat, with a hump to support the rider from behind. Shorter than the standard seat, it retained the hinged mountings and was long and sufficiently well-padded for comfort over long race distances. Footrests were rear-set items with a new brake pedal to suit. The gear-change pedal was reversed so it could be reached from the newly-sited right footrest. This reversed the gear-change pattern to 'down for up' – preferred by many racers – but the traditional Triumph 'up for up' pattern could be restored by reversing the cam-plate inside the gearbox.

A further seven racing Bonnevilles were built for 1966, for entry in events by Meriden's favoured dealers. Their engines featured an internal oil feed for the exhaust cam, their wheels had alloy rims, the colour scheme was now Grenadier Red and Alaskan White, and a sleeker 'nosecone' Avon Fairing was fitted.

Production racing was introduced at the Isle of Man TT races in 1967, when the 750cc class was won by John Hartle on one of four T120 racers created for factory use from T120TTs taken off the line in December 1966. By this point any pretence that these were not works specials had been

dropped and the 1967 build boasted modernised seats and fairings, alternative front brakes, huge alloy fuel tanks and – on some machines – 1³⁄₁₆in Amal GP racing carburettors. While such goodies were listed in a leaflet entitled High Performance Alternative Parts, they were virtually impossible to obtain through dealers.

Intensifying Production Class competition saw the factory racers being fitted with new crankcases, or even new engines, as necessary. They ultimately gave 58bhp but had reached their reliability limit and were replaced in 1970 by 750cc Trident triples.

Triumph Bonnevilles won the annual 500-Miler in 1961 and consecutively from 1965 to 1969. Factory entries won the 750cc Production TT in 1967 and in 1969, when winner Malcolm Uphill averaged 99.99mph for the three-lap (113-mile) event and recorded one lap at 100.37mph, the first at over 100mph by a Production Class machine on the TT Mountain Course. In the same year, Uphill and co-rider Steve Jolly won their class at the Barcelona 24 Hours endurance race on a Bonneville.

Only 30 or so genuine Thruxton Bonnevilles of any type are believed to survive today.

Oil tank with cutaway (above left) – to clear carburettor intake – was a listed Thruxton part. Shapely alloy fuel tank (above right) holds five Imperial gallons and features Monza quick-release filler cap.

Late works-style Thruxton glass-fibre racing seat (far left) made for Triumph by Screen & Plastics. On 1965 and 1966 builds, hinged steel racing seat with overall black vinyl covering was fitted. Long Thruxton silencers (left) are supported at their rear ends by bracing straps to the frame.

Chapter 7

Oil-in-frame T120s & the T140: 1971-74

Entering the 1970s, the BSA Group faced a stiff challenge as the Japanese industry geared up to produce ever larger, faster and more sophisticated motorcycles. Unfortunately, attempts at Group reorganisation that went awry were to have far-reaching consequences for the Bonneville, which was no longer the fastest machine on the market.

A particularly damaging move was the hasty introduction of a new frame shared by 650 twins of both the BSA and Triumph marques. Added to this, there was a wholesale redesign of cycle parts by Group staff, some of them with little motorcycle industry experience, working at a facility

remote from Meriden. The 1971 Bonneville was not only late reaching showrooms: its new looks and high build put buyers off.

With high-performance Japanese machines now flooding on to both the home and US markets, the decision was taken to enlarge the Bonneville's engine to create a 750 version, which emerged for 1973. The new T140 twin had an actual displacement of 744cc, after an early run of machines was released at 724cc. Triumph had originally designed the three-cylinder T150 as its 750cc Bonneville replacement, but this proved to be a slow seller and demand for a twin remained

A 1972 US five-speed T120RV model. In the absence of an oil tank, there are combined side panel and air filter housings.

strong. Boosting to 750cc a 1930s engine design that had started at 500cc was clearly a case of hopeful evolution rather than progress on the Japanese scale, but for 1973 two Bonnevilles were offered: the 650 T120 and the 750 T140V.

In October 1973, as production of the 1974 models was getting under way, all work at Meriden suddenly stopped when the factory was occupied by a sizeable section of the workforce. BSA-Triumph's struggling motorcycle operations had been merged into the Norton Villiers Group to form Norton Villiers Triumph, and the protest came about following an announcement that Meriden was scheduled to close early in 1974. Group head Dennis Poore's plan was to concentrate all NVT production at two factories: BSA's Small Heath works in Birmingham and Norton's plant in Wolverhampton.

Only a handful of 1974 Bonnevilles were completed before the sit-in, and, as events turned out, they would not be released for sale until the late summer of 1974. After a Meriden Worker's Co-operative was formed, output eventually resumed

in March 1975, when a few more 1974 models were produced before a very short 1975 production run started.

Engine
1971

The 1971 season, starting at engine number NE 01436, was most notable for the re-design of the cycle parts. However, there were a number of engine modifications, some of which were dictated by the chassis alterations. Revised cylinder head and rocker boxes were required before the engine would even fit in the new oil-bearing Group frame. Four locating dowels were used to fit the rocker boxes, which had to be milled internally to give sufficient clearance for assembly. The four head bolts also holding down the rocker boxes were now in two sections, the first holding the head to the cylinder block before the second section threaded inside it to secure the rocker box.

Pushrod tubes changed again, the lower ends reverting to the 1969 layout, having a pressed-in

A 1974 Bonneville in US specification: this machine was originally supplied to a UK customer.

From 1972 rocker boxes feature one-piece inspection caps as seen on this 1974 T120R. Twin downtubes of duplex oil-bearing frame show well.

collar containing a double O-ring and silicone sealing washer. At the top, three small holes provided oil drainage in place of the castellations previously employed.

In the bottom end, the crankshaft got a revised flywheel, now attached by stronger bolts with flat washers. At the drive-side end of the crankshaft, a new engine sprocket – without a ground face to bear against the oil seal – appeared, and so did a revised distance piece to complement adjusting shims that were now used for fine adjustment of the primary chain alignment. The oil seal on the drive side of the crank was also deleted.

The crankcase came in for some revision too. A new oil pressure relief valve with UNF threads was fitted, but, despite the new thread forms, it could be fitted to earlier Bonnevilles without modification. After engine number GE 27029, a world shortage of bearings forced an unsatisfactory switch to a metric-sized timing-side main bearing. Not only did the crankcase casting have to be machined to accept this, but the right-side crankshaft journal and timing pinion nut had to be modified too.

Again as a result of the new rolling chassis, the exhaust system was all-new for 1971. The downpipes looked similar to those of the previous models, but the silencers were very different. For both home-market and US Bonnevilles, long megaphone-shaped silencers took a big step away from Triumph's traditional shape.

1972

Early 1972 models, starting from engine number HG 30870, were little changed except for new bigend bearing cap nuts. Later in the season, however, wider-section timing pinions with threaded holes to accommodate pullers were fitted and the oil pressure relief valve reverted to the earlier two-part type after engine number CG 50464. From engine number XG 42304, a new cylinder head casting appeared. It was designed to accept bolt-on inlet port adaptors, and the exhaust ports lost their stubs and featured machined recesses to take push-in pipes. More for style than any real need, finned cast-alloy clamps were fitted to the exhaust pipes where they entered the head.

Along with the new head, new rocker box castings for both the inlet and exhaust side dispensed with the separate inspection covers in favour of two longer, finned covers, and new two-piece holding-down bolts were also specified.

1973

The T120, starting from engine number JH 15366, continued unchanged, except for colour schemes, through 1973. The major changes were reserved for the new T140V model, which was introduced at engine number JH 15435.

At first, the T140V's increased capacity was achieved by simply boring out the existing cylinder block to 75mm, which, combined with the original stroke of 82mm, resulted in an engine of 724cc. Curiously the cylinder head on these early T140s featured two different thread types for the cylinder head bolts: the four outer bolts were the old Cycle Engineer's thread type, while the four inner bolts were UNF. From engine number XH 22019, a new cylinder block casting with Unified threads allowed the bore to be increased to 76mm, giving a displacement of 744cc. This was to be the Bonneville's final engine capacity.

The new block was shorter, requiring shorter con rods. This had the benefit of making it possible to install the engine in the frame with the rocker boxes in place. A later cylinder casting, which appeared at engine number CH 29520, retained the 76mm bore but also benefited from two central $\frac{5}{16}$in head-fixing bolts, bringing the total number of head bolts to ten. At the same time, the oilways were opened up to increase flow, new valve guides were specified and the cylinder head steady was changed to a flat strip attached to the centre rocker box studs. In the US, 8.6:1 pistons became standard, but in the UK the compression ratio was kept down to 7.9:1.

Naturally there was some revision of the bottom end. A new crankshaft with a balance factor of 74 per cent kept the old flywheel, but with yet another revised set of bolts. Hepolite pistons with reinforced crowns and three-part oil control rings, together with stronger and thicker gudgeon pins, were attached to the strengthened con rods and a larger timing-side main bearing was fitted. The shorter block meant that pushrods and their tubes were shortened to suit.

To cope with increased power and the potential for increased vibration, the crankcase was strengthened. A wider mouth was needed to clear the enlarged bores and the bearing bosses were thickened considerably.

A mix of fierce inlet and milder exhaust cam profiles made the engine less torquey than it could have been, but reduced vibration and prolonged main bearing life.

Exhausts were unchanged at the start of the year, but at engine number AH 22965 a longer 'torpedo' silencer with a curved reverse cone at its end appeared. Rarely seen today, this was rapidly superseded by a design with a longer, straight-sided reverse cone, which remained on the Bonneville until the end of Meriden production.

1974

Starting from engine number GJ 55101, there were only detail modifications to the Bonneville in 1974, partially because the actual production

'V', the Roman numeral for '5', under the Bonneville name denotes fitment of five-speed gearbox, new for 1972.

Tapered silencer and conical alloy rear hub were both part of major restyling for 1971, seen on a 1972 US T120RV.

run was so small and the usual stream of mid-season revisions did not occur. The most significant change was new rocker boxes with two extra fixing points for the inspection covers. The oil pressure relief valve gained a finer mesh filter and a new oil pressure sensor and rubber cover were also fitted.

Fuel system & carburettors

1971
No changes were made to the 30mm Amal Concentric carburettors, although new mesh and felt air filters appeared, in a cast alloy housing behind the carburettors. Rubber hoses joined the carburettor inlets to the new filter box.

1972
The carburettors remained unchanged, but had new bolt-on alloy flange adaptors connecting them to the new cylinder head.

1973
Amal Type 390 30mm Concentric carburettors continued to be fitted to both T120 and T140, although they now had 210 main jets. Carburettor inlet manifolds, however, were new for 1973. A balance tube was still fitted between the two straight 1⅛in inlets, but the left side now carried a tapped mounting for the choke lever. The carburettors breathed through new separate air filters housed in new covers.

1974
No changes were listed for the 1974 season.

Transmission
1971
No gearbox changes were recorded for 1971, although from April an optional five-speed Quaife gearbox conversion was listed, featuring a roller bearing on the sleeve gear. Originally an aftermarket item adopted by the factory's race team, the conversion was designed to fit without altering existing components – and with a few modifications it could also be fitted to earlier machines. Later in the season, the clutch shock absorber centre assembly was strengthened.

1972
Changes here were confined to revisions affecting the three-ball clutch lifting mechanism. The five-speed gear cluster was still available as an option.

1973
Although the engine of the T120 was unchanged, its primary transmission benefited from improvements introduced for the T140. A ⅜in triplex chain replaced the duplex item and the chaincase cover was redesigned to suit the wider drive. Stiffer clutch springs and a revised clutch shock absorber spider were also fitted.

In the gearbox, the five-speed cluster fitted to the T140V was not without its problems. A new high gear assembly and layshaft featured a high gear pinion retained by a circlip rather than being just pressed on to the shaft. Notwithstanding this, the T140V had a tendency to jump out of gear, so, to combat this, a conversion kit – produced mid-season – provided replacement first, second and third gear layshaft pinions, first and second gear mainshaft pinions, a layshaft first gear selector fork and a layshaft drive dog. It was not so much a conversion kit as a new gearbox but, allied to the adoption of a gearchange camplate and indexing plunger from the T150 Trident, it effected a cure.

1974

The gearbox final drive sprocket received a cham-fered face to suit the new locknut and washer, which incorporated an 'O' ring to combat oil leaking past the splines. On the back of the primary drive case, the fitting for the breather hose was replaced by a plastic item.

Frame & rear suspension

1971

Out went the old lugged and brazed frame and swinging arm, and in came the all-welded oil-bearing structure devised at the Group's Umber-slade Hall research and development facility.

The heart of this new frame was a 3in diameter main tube, which ran back from the steering head before curving sharply down to form the seat post. This doubled as a 4-pint oil tank for which a filler neck was provided just before the point at which the tube curved downwards.

Originally the filler had been sited immedi-ately behind the steering head, providing a more adequate oil capacity, but it was apparently feared that riders might mistake it for the fuel filler. At the base of the main tube, a detachable sump plate with drain plug and wire screen filter was fitted. Initially, the plate and filter were in one piece, but later models benefited from their separation, which eased servicing.

Running from the steering head were twin down-tubes that echoed the old duplex frames of the early 1960s. The frame number stamping was now at the top of the left downtube. The twin tubes formed a cradle under the engine before curving up to support the swinging arm and meet the rear seat loop.

Welded-on loops for the rear footrests branched off the tubes just aft of the swinging arm mounting plate, while a cross-bracing tube linked the bottom tubes under the power unit. The seat loop narrowed at its forward end to meet the main spine just behind the oil filler neck, where it was strength-ened with a broad gusset.

A 1972 T120RV in US trim. Forks with alloy sliders and four-stud caps were introduced with the oil-bearing frame. Colours are Tiger Gold over Cold White.

The frame demanded all-new ancillaries. Engine plates, rear brake pedal, footrests, chainguard and stands were all totally changed for 1971. At the rear, suspension was now controlled by firmer 110lb/in Girling shock absorbers with much closer-pitched chromed coils.

A new 'Made in England' transfer appeared on the frame's right-side downtube in 1971. One could be forgiven for thinking that it had been introduced much earlier, looking at the many restored pre-1971 Triumphs that display this popular decal today.

1972

Recognising the unpopularity of the excessive seat height, the Triumph factory set out to rectify it by attaching the rear subframe to the seat post nearly 3in further down. Together with modifications to forks, rear shocks and seat, they managed to reduce seat height to an acceptable 32½in. But stocks of the old tall frame had to be used up first,

and it was not until engine number CG 50414 that the new type reached production. Prior to that, narrowing and lowering of the front of the seat (achieved by removing some of its padding), together with shortening the forks, had been the interim solution.

This 'quick fix' had the unfortunate effect of tipping the whole machine forwards, which meant fuel at the low front end of the tank could not make it to the fuel taps, and probably affected the steering characteristics.

The modified frame demanded alterations to the rear suspension, so shorter Girling shock absorbers levelled the machine out again and restored the full use of the fuel tank. Lowering the subframe also entailed revising the battery carrier, air filter box, ignition coil mountings and side panels. An extra cross-brace appeared under the seat and the side reflectors at the rear now mounted on tabs welded direct to the frame. The swinging arm was unchanged.

Few 1974 machines left Meriden before the factory was blockaded by a significant section of the workforce from October 1973. This US model has the long silencers and side panel badges first fitted in 1973. Colours are Regal Purple with Cold White.

1973

Changes to the frame were few. The seat hinges were relocated to the left side, although the earliest 1973 T140s had 1972-type frames with right-side hinges. The seat gained its familiar plunger-type securing catch, the oil filler cap in the integral frame tube oil tank gained a dipstick permanently attached to its underside, and the fairing lugs disappeared from the front of the steering head. The rear shock absorbers were now ½in shorter to assist in lowering the seat height.

1974

No changes were listed for the 1974 season.

Steering & front suspension

1971

With the new frame came a new fork. With looks leaning heavily towards the contemporary Italian Ceriani type, the new assembly now pivoted on tapered roller bearings and dispensed with the traditional rubber gaiters. Hard chrome-plated stanchions slid in cast-alloy sliders, the fork seals protected only by rubber dust excluders. Internal springs controlled the 6in of travel the new forks afforded and new internals effected two-way damping. At the bottom of the sliders the front wheel spindle was now retained by alloy caps, secured by four studs on each side. At the top of the fork, yokes finished in black enamel gripped the stanchions and provided the mounting points for chromed wire headlamp and instrument brackets. Early 1971 machines suffered from premature fork seal failure, so improved seals were fitted later in the year.

All-new Lucas switchgear, consisting of units which incorporated pivots for the alloy ball-ended control levers, also appeared for 1971. The pivots were drilled to accept rear-view mirrors, which were not supplied as standard equipment. The choke lever was now a separate unit located on the right side of the handlebar.

1972

A new bottom yoke, with the steering stem thread changed from 16 to 24 UNF thread, appeared at the same time as the shorter fork. Shortening both the stanchions and springs achieved the desired height reduction at the front of the machine.

1973

The rear suspension did not change much, but the front did. The Trident, which had already donated a number of components to the T140V, provided the latest Bonneville's fork featuring polished alloy sliders, hard chromed stanchions, internal springs and new cast-iron yokes in black enamel.

Two-piece sheet metal shrouds were again

placed at the top of the forks between the top and bottom yokes, featuring rubber-mounted headlamp brackets and, on the left side, the ignition switch mounting. Shrouds on UK models were finished in black while US machines got chrome. As in 1972, US stanchions went naked, but UK models wore protective rubber gaiters without clips. On the left-side slider the most significant modification was a cast-on mounting bracket for the Lockheed hydraulic disc brake.

At the top of the new forks, handlebars with revised bends for all markets kept the brake master cylinder level. US machines received 8in-rise 'bars, while UK machines had more traditional low 'bars. With the new arrangement on the carburettor manifold, the choke lever disappeared from the handlebars.

1974

After a long run, the optional steering damper was finally deleted from the parts lists, while the forks now sported strengthened mudguard mounting brackets on their sliders.

Wheels, brakes & tyres

1971

New wheels were among the many innovations for 1971. Alloy racer-style conical hubs, with pressed-in liners for the brake drums, wore a 19in steel rim at the front and an 18in size at the rear. Tyres were 3.25 x 19in front and 4.00 x 18in rear Dunlop K70s for all markets.

Although it was still an 8in twin-leading-shoe design, the entirely redesigned front brake was very different from its predecessor – and not as

The often-reviled conical hub twin-leading-shoe drum brake fitted to early oil-in-frame models. It is not as effective as the type fitted from 1968 to 1970, but can work well if carefully restored and adjusted.

New in 1973 was the single hydraulic front disc brake, with Lockheed caliper and 10in plated iron rotor.

Rear brake details show brake arm arrangement (above) as used from 1971 until the arrival of the rear disc brake in 1976, and brake light switch layout (below) for oil-in-frame machines.

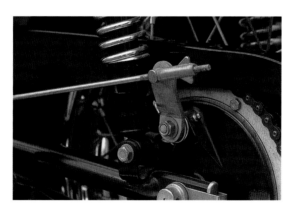

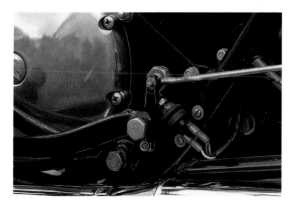

powerful. Two short operating arms now turned the cams in opposite directions to each other, rather than together. The backplate featured a large air scoop at the front with two exit vents at the bottom. It also had a rubber-capped access hole through which the brake shoes could be adjusted. Later in the year, a spring replaced the rubber boot between the operating arms after problems with the cable becoming unseated from its locating point in the backplate.

At the rear, a 7in brake drum no longer had fully-floating shoes. It received a thicker liner during the year, along with a longer, upward-pointing operating arm with a heavier return spring and thicker fulcrum pads. A 47-tooth final drive sprocket lowered overall gearing.

1972
There were no changes to the wheels, brakes and tyres for 1972.

1973
The introduction of a front disc brake entailed several front wheel changes. The 10in-diameter, chrome-plated, cast-iron disc was bolted to a two-piece alloy hub, but rim size remained at 19in with a 3.25-section Dunlop K70 tyre as before. Bolted to the new left-side fork slider casting was a cast-iron, single-piston caliper activated from the master cylinder on the right handlebar via a mixture of steel brake lines and flexible hose. The top fork yoke incorporated a lug onto which the junction between the master cylinder hose and the upper portion of the brake line was mounted. The caliper's chromed cover bore a circular 'Triumph Hydraulic' sticker. It is worth noting that although the disc brake's performance was superior to the conical hub's, the chrome plating on the rotor was prone to peel off, whereupon brake pad life became very brief indeed.

At the rear, a downward pointing brake-operating arm with a square tapered fit on to a revised cam was fitted in mid-season. US rear tyres went up a size to 4.25 x 18in.

1974
No changes were listed for the 1974 season.

Seat & bodywork
1971
A new seat was necessitated by the change of frame. It was well-padded, but shorter than the old version. Finished in black with the Triumph name in gold on the rear, the cover had the same aerated vinyl ridges as before, but now lacked the step separating the rider and passenger portions.

Rather flimsy, welded, L-shaped hinges on the right and an over-centre catch on the left meant that the seat now opened in the opposite direction to previous models. Although the seat was comfortable in itself, many riders found its height of 34in off the road excessive and awkward. This problem was addressed by a series of minor seat and frame modifications.

A redesigned fuel tank was required for the oil-bearing frame. Early 1971 machines all had the same 3½-gallon (US measure) tank regardless of market. Not until later in the year was the larger, slab-sided 4-gallon (Imperial measure) version fitted to UK machines. Early-season tanks were of similar shape to the earlier Triumph type but slightly wider at the front, and featured a BSA-type centre mounting bolt with rubber saddles on the spinal tube providing lateral stability. A black rubber plug filled the hole in the centre of the tank, while a central chrome strip bent under the tank at either end was clamped by a circular chrome trim around the central mounting bolt.

Tank finish was Tiger Gold and black with white pinstriping. All the early-shape tanks had a Tiger Gold base coat with black flashes curving rearwards from both top and bottom of the tank badge. The 4-gallon UK tanks were Tiger Gold with a black surround on the sides and a broad black stripe running down the centre of the tank top, separated from the Tiger Gold by white pin-striping. Instead of 1969-style badges, the boxy 'bread bin' tank, as it became known, had plain Triumph logos in black and chrome. Transfers were as in 1970.

Mudguards were, once again, painted steel, but were much shorter than previously. At the front, the guard was supported by thin wire front and rear stays that clamped to threaded bosses on the fork sliders. Support was minimal, so an extra centre stay was added later in the year. A chromed combined stay and grab rail supported the rear mudguard and US models carried a pair of red side reflectors on each side to complement the amber ones on the front frame downtube. Both mudguards were finished in Tiger Gold, with a black centre stripe and white pinstripes.

As the frame carried the engine oil, no separate tank was necessary. In its place was a combined air filter box in alloy with pressed-steel side panels rearward of it. The right side panel housed a combined ignition and lighting switch, and provided concealment for the Zener diode and its heat sink. Between the two side panels a redesigned battery carrier was joined behind the main frame tube by a rubber-bushed vertical mounting for the two ignition coils. Both side panels and the air filter box were in plain black, although the right-hand panel bore a 'Bonneville' transfer in gold.

1972

The slimming of the seat has already been described in the section about the frame and rear suspension. The front mudguard was still the late 1971 version with the extra centre stay, while the rear guard was unchanged.

Colours for 1972 were Tiger Gold with a Cold White centre stripe, lined in black. Fuel tanks again varied according to market, although UK tanks could be specified by US customers and vice versa. US tanks were unchanged except for their

colour schemes, of which there were two for 1972. Both featured the same colours, but with different designs. The first and most common design was Tiger Gold above Cold White, with the white starting from the top edge of the tank badge. From there, it ran forward to the front of the tank, dividing it more or less in half horizontally. At the rear of the badge, the white curved down and rearwards below the knee-grip rubber and continued in a narrow strip to the rear edge of the tank. The second US design featured a Tiger Gold tank with two flashes of Cold White on either side. One of these started from the bottom of the tank badge and was the width of its lower edge. This curved down and rearwards to the bottom edge of the tank. At the top of the badge, a flash of similar width tapered upwards before curving sharply back and finishing in a point. The larger UK tanks were Tiger Gold with Cold White for the centre

Tank patterns and colours – this 1972 US scheme is Tiger Gold over Cold White – continued to change most years. Tank secures to oil-bearing frame with a single central bolt, under weatherproofing bung.

Seat for 1973 and 1974 had a slightly raised pillion section and chromed trim around its base. Stainless steel mudguard and 'five speed' sticker are correct for this 1974 model.

Close up of the screw-on
side panel badge used
from 1973.

Close up of the screw-on side panel badge used from 1973.

stripe and lower side borders. Pinstriping between the colours was black and triangular rubber knee-grips were fitted.

The headlamp shell remained chrome, while the rear lamp housing stayed silver painted.

Air filter boxes and side panels were in black, and wore new clear plastic stickers with the Bonneville name in gold with a border in the same colour. The lettering style had changed too, into a decorative typeface typical of the 1970s. On five-speed models a 'V' was added in gold below the 'Bonneville' box. Later in the year, a separate round sticker on the rear mudguard re-affirmed the presence of five speeds.

1973

The seat reverted to having a slightly raised rear section that delineated separate seating areas for rider and passenger. The ribbed and aerated top

New rear-end features: direction indicators were standard from 1971, this type of tail light was used from 1971 to 1973, and side reflector is the type seen on 1971 and early 1972 machines.

remained, as did the all-black finish and Triumph logo applied to the rear, but there was now a bright chrome trim on the lower edge. At the rear, the new seat tipped up slightly and its sides were covered in a slightly coarser textured material.

Mudguards were, thankfully, longer than the truncated 1972 versions and were finished in polished chrome plate except on T120 models, whose cycle parts were unchanged from the previous year. The new chromed guards on 750 models reverted to 'pre-oil-in-frame' style, with stays between the rear of the guard and lugs on the lower fork sliders.

Fuel tanks on 650 and 750 models remained the same in the UK, although the 750s wore the new season's colour scheme while the 650s made do with the previous year's scheme. The base colour for 1973 was Hi-Fi Vermilion with a panel in Gold on the sides of the tank. This covered most of the front half of the tank's side, surrounding a new cast 'Triumph' badge, and extended back over the top of the knee-grip, following its downward curve and tapering to a point, roughly in line with the rear edge of the knee-grip. Pinstriping was in white.

As the fuel tank was now the only showcase for colour, it was easier to change colour schemes for different markets. Canadian models for 1973, for example, were finished in Astral Red and Silver, while the home-market 650s made do with left-over 1972 colours and US models were Purple and Cold White. This is confusing enough, but, in addition, US models now got as standard the slimline 2½-gallon (US measure) tank that had become available to dealers unpainted at the end of 1972. Visually, the only difference between the 650 and 750 models in the USA was the colour of the tank and the silver-on-red, embossed plastic badge on the new, black plastic side panel/air filter box. Colours on US T140RVs were the same as the UK 750s, but with the Gold secondary colour being confined to the two flashes running upwards from the top edge of the tank badge, before curving back and tapering to a point towards the rear of the tank.

1974

The only significant changes for 1974 were to colours, although in the US the 2½-gallon (US measure) slimline fuel tank was replaced by a 3.6-gallon (US measure) version. On the side panels, the embossed 'Bonneville 650' and 'Bonneville 750' badges were standardised, with gold lettering on a black background now being used for all models. Fuel tank graphics were unchanged, but the colours were now Purple and Cold White for the T120 models and Cherokee Red and Cold White for the larger machines, with gold pinstriping on all.

Electrics
1971
Since they had been re-sited, the ignition coils now had longer HT leads with smaller Champion WC200 insulating caps. A new four-position key-operated ignition switch was specified, and the ignition capacitors were now housed between the ignition coils.

The most obvious changes were the introduction of flashing direction indicators and the new alloy Lucas switchgear. On the left handlebar, one cluster controlled the horn, dipswitch and head-lamp flasher, while on the right the indicator switch and ignition cut-out were to be found. The indicators had amber lenses fixed in chromed housings. At the front they were mounted on hollow, chromed stems that also fastened the headlamp shell to its wire bracket. The rear indicators were similar, but mounted through the sides of a sheet metal rear light assembly.

A shallower 'flat-back' headlamp shell now housed the Lucas unit along with warning lamps for ignition and main beam, plus an indicator repeater. No ammeter was fitted. At the rear, a new Lucas L679 stop and tail light was mounted to the mudguard by a new bracket arrangement. A single Lucas 6H horn faced forwards beneath the front of the fuel tank and a new plastic rear stop light switch, mounted directly to the frame, was actuated by the brake pedal. By now, the wiring loom was plastic rather than fabric covered, while headlamp bulb wattage fell from 50/40W to 45/35W.

1972
A new, louder Lucas 6H horn appeared, and shorter front indicator stems, like those on the T150 Trident, were fitted. In response to demand from customers and press alike, the positions of the handlebar switches were reversed for 1972. The indicator, headlight flasher and cut-out switches were all now on the left, while the dip-switch and horn moved to the right along with the still function-less bottom switch with which they shared a housing.

1973
Lucas 10CA contact breaker points and a new auto-advance unit were fitted to all 1973 models. The combined ignition and lighting switch intro-duced in 1971 was abandoned. The key-operated ignition switch was re-sited in the left-hand head-lamp bracket and a two-position lighting switch was placed on the headlamp shell, as in 1970.

At the front of the machine, the headlamp shell reverted to the earlier, deeper style, allowing more space for the three warning lamps and a new three-position toggle switch for the lights. Longer

indicator stems, as used on the T150 Trident, made these lights more visible in use. A cast-alloy housing bolted to the rear mudguard carried the new stop and tail lamp introduced as a result of US legislation, while the rear indicators were moved out on to the grab rail gusset, giving them equal prominence with the front ones.

1974
No changes were listed for the 1974 season.

Instruments
1971
A new Smiths 150mph speedometer and an unchanged tachometer now sat in vibration-proofing rubber cups in the wire brackets above the top yoke.

1972
Both speedometer and rev counter remained the same as for the previous year.

1973
Both the speedometer and tachometer continued unchanged, although their chromed pressed-sheet supports were now secured to the fork tops by an extra chromed outer fork cap nut.

1974
No changes were listed for the 1974 season.

Lucas switchgear on 1974 T120R looks primitive compared with that on the Bonneville's Japanese contemporaries.

Chapter 8

Meriden Co-operative T140s: 1975-79

The first of the 1975-season Bonnevilles, which had engine number DK 6100, was actually completed in April of that year, and was the first machine to be manufactured by the new Workers' Co-operative formed by staff in occupation at the Meriden plant. Prior to that, some 1974 models that were standing incomplete in the factory had been finished and despatched. With no opportunity for development during the shutdown, the 1975 models were identical to the 1974 machines in every respect: the only way to tell the two years' production apart is by reference to the engine numbers. Because of the late start on 1975 models, they were produced for only two months.

Brochure shot of the home market T140 for 1976, first year of the left-side gearchange and rear disc brake.

After 17 years, the 649cc Bonneville was dropped for 1976 as the Co-op saw its uncertain future best served by the bigger T140 twin. From 1976, the men at Meriden concentrated on the US market, where there was most sales potential for what was increasingly being seen as an ageing engine design. This policy, however, meant continuing compliance with ever tighter US emission and safety controls.

Bonnevilles for 1977 were unchanged in technical specification, but there were differences in finish for the standard T140V and, notably, on the special T140J Silver Jubilee model. To coincide with celebrations in Britain marking the 25th year of Queen Elizabeth II's reign, Meriden hit on the idea of a special edition of the Bonneville. Its distinctive trim featured silver, as well as patriotic red, white and blue.

Originally it was announced that the Jubilee Bonneville would be made in a limited edition of 1000 and the first batch's side panel badges bore the legend 'One of a Thousand'. However, demand for the machine was sufficient to persuade the Co-

The Jubilee Bonneville of 1977 – although not in gleaming condition this is a little-used UK model. Only three miles are recorded on the speedometer of this Jubilee, unaltered since leaving the factory.

operative to release a further 1000 T140Js for the US market, with the wording altered to read 'Limited Edition'. A further batch, generally agreed to have been about 400, was produced for

UK-specification T140D bought new by Essex owner Dennis Middleton from Surrey dealer Carl Rosner in 1979. Non-Triumph period fairing and luggage were fitted for Dennis before he took delivery.

general export. Each machine was sold with a certificate of authenticity, which differed between the US and UK markets.

The Jubilee appealed to collectors who wanted a machine as much for ornament as for riding, or as a sentimental souvenir of a British motorcycle industry which in 1977 looked set for extinction. As a result, a high proportion of T140Js have remained in totally original condition. All the Jubilee's variations from standard were cosmetic.

The T140V's final year was 1978, when the new T140E was introduced, initially for the USA only. The E suffix signified compliance with new regulations introduced by the Environmental Protection Agency (EPA) in that country. Applied to vehicles manufactured after 1 January 1978, the regulations prohibited crankcase and oil tank breathers from venting into the atmosphere.

The 1979 model year saw the introduction of the new T140D Special, which joined the T140E in Triumph's two-model line-up. Designed specifically at the request of American dealers, the 'D Special' was Triumph's response to the growing

trend for marketing ready-customised machines. Said to have been planned as a limited edition, the T140D was actually made in reasonable quantity, relative to the small output of the underfinanced Co-operative, running at 200 units a week in 1979.

Engine

1976
Production for 1976, the first full season of output for the Co-op, began at engine number HN 62501. O-rings were added at the revised timing inspection cover on the primary chaincase and at the pressure-release valve. There were also revisions to the oil pipes and their associated junction block. The silencers' end-cones now featured almost parallel taper and there were internal noise-reducing revisions.

1977
Engine numbers on the Jubilee followed the same sequence as standard T140V models but with a J

suffix after the V. For 1977, engine numbers began at GP 75000. Although there were no internal differences from 1976 models, there were alterations to external finish for the Jubilee. All outer engine cases, primary drive cover, gearbox outer cover and timing cover were finished in bright chromium plate, applied on the aluminium alloy.

1978

At the start of the year, production was based on the existing T140V model with a few minor revisions. Starting at engine number HX 00100, compression ratio was standardised at 7.9:1 for all markets. While this was helpful in terms of reliability and oil tightness, it did nothing for the 750cc Bonneville's increasingly lacklustre performance. A new design of composite head gasket replaced the venerable solid copper item, and, from engine number 02690, rockers and adjusters received UNF threads. A lock-washer under the alternator rotor nut and revisions to timing marks on the cam pinions were the only other changes.

The changeover to production of the T140E, which took place in time for the 1 January 1978 deadline, marked the end of one of the Bonneville's enduring trademarks – the splayed-port cylinder head. A new casting featured parallel inlet tracts with stub mountings for the carburettors. It also had a reshaped combustion chamber, and was fitted with new iron valve guides and revised valve spring cups.

Crankcase pressure was still directed into the primary case, from where the breather recycled into the airbox rather than venting to atmosphere at the rear of the machine. Similarly, the oil tank breather was re-routed to the exhaust rockerbox.

1979

Very little in the way of engine modifications took place for 1979, when production started with engine number HA 11001. The E engine continued largely unchanged in both T140D Special and T140E Bonneville models. Phillips-head screws gave way to more practical Allen type for securing the outer covers and a gasket was employed between the timing cover and crankcase.

The T140D Special sported an all-new two-into-one exhaust system, which exited through a silencer unique to the model. Tapered along roughly half of its length, it was chrome-plated and had an annular arrangement at its rear outlet. From the cylinder head, the two downpipes tucked in towards each other, joining in a junction box just below the front frame downtube. There was no balance pipe and bracing straps bolting to the engine ran from tabs welded to the downpipes. At the cylinder head, the pipes were flanged and held into the threaded ports by a screw-in collar with integral cooling fins.

Fuel system & carburettors

1976

By now, the Bonneville's 30mm Amal carburettors were being made at the company's Spanish plant and for 1976 they gained extensions to the tickler buttons. Induction noise was muted by an intake silencer tube introduced through the centre of each air filter, and new petrol taps were now clearly marked with 'on' and 'off' positions as required by US legislation.

1977

No changes were listed for the 1977 season.

1978

No changes were recorded for the T140V, but induction on the US-market T140E was now through a pair of 30mm Amal Concentric MkII

Outer engine covers (top) are chromium-plated on the Jubilee variant. The plate, applied on aluminium alloy, tends to deteriorate on all but the most pampered machines. Back to a normal engine finish (above) for the T140D. Side panel badges were specific to this model.

This T140J has been owned from new by Bill Crosby, proprietor of Reg Allen, a London Triumph shop which kept strong links with Meriden until closure. A variant was produced for the USA and a high proportion of the 2400 made were retained by dealers or have been preserved as collector's items. Left-foot gearchange became standardised from 1976 to suit US regulations.

carburettors. Outwardly, their 'square' appearance looked a world apart from the earlier instrument, henceforth known as the MkI. Apart from a lever-operated cold-start device to replace the 'dirty' ticklers and a new finish on the throttle slides, however, they were little changed in function. Mounted on the body of the left-hand carburettor, the lever enriched both carburettors at once by means of a linkage

1979

No changes were listed for the 1979 season.

Transmission

1976

This was the major area of change in 1976, when demands for standardisation in the US market forced the adoption of a left-foot gearchange. This

meant a host of new parts and castings for the T140. A cross-over shaft, which was cranked to clear the clutch, passed through the rear of the gearbox casing and emerged with a splined end near the centre of the primary drive cover.

The change entailed new inner and outer gearbox covers, a bush for the gearchange shaft, a revised gearchange quadrant and new kick-start shaft. The redesigned primary chaincase now had a smaller screw-in plug with two large crossed slots on its face. The Triumph name still appeared on the cover, embossed below the inspection plug.

1977

No changes were listed for the 1977 season.

1978

A gasket was introduced between gearbox inner and outer covers on both the T140V and T140E.

1979

A new gearbox camplate provided a more positive neutral selection simply by making the neutral location notch deeper. A raised button on the camplate now actuated, somewhat erratically, a neutral warning lamp at the handlebars.

Frame & rear suspension

1976

The frame was modified to accept components required for both the new rear disc brake and revised gearshift. The swinging arm now gained a mounting plate for the rear brake's caliper while the rider's footrests were now the same part on each side rather than the 'handed' rests previously fitted. The folding pillion footrests were angled 45 degrees rearwards to comply with US legislation.

Provision was made on the frame for mounting a master cylinder for the rear brake, which entailed amending the battery carrier and ignition coil mountings. The rear suspension units were unchanged but one new exhaust mounting bracket was required to clear the rear brake hose.

1977

No changes were made to the T140V, but the Jubilee introduced 'upside-down' Girling gas-filled rear shock absorbers fitted with their pre-load adjusters uppermost. Like the standard oil-damped units, they featured chromed springs.

Probably wisely, the factory opted not to change the black enamelled finish of the Jubilee's frame and swinging arm.

1978

No changes were made to the frame but the two pillion footrests were now different for each side instead of being identical, due to a mounting bolt revision. Rear suspension units were replaced mid-season by the chromed, gas-assisted units seen on the Jubilee Bonneville.

1979

The steering head was slightly modified to accommodate the repositioned steering security lock, which was moved from the top yoke to the underside of the bottom yoke to allow space for the new ignition switch and warning lamp panel.

A plate welded to the top rail of the rear frame loop on the right allowed Bonneville owners to lock their hinged seat for the first time. Footrest rubbers ceased to be interchangeable, with different left and right rubbers being specified. The round rubbers were replaced by items with a squarer shape, moulded-in ribs on the top surfaces and chamfered outer ends. At the rear, a small chrome rack was now fitted as standard, forming part of the rear mudguard support stay.

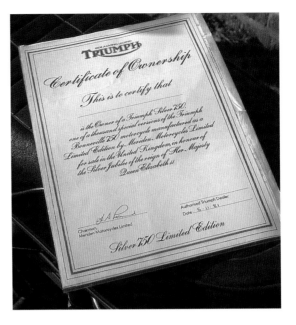

Certificate of authenticity issued with UK Jubilee models. US documents were slightly more elaborate than the UK version, and embossed.

Patriotic red, white and blue livery everywhere on the Jubilee – even on the chromed wheel rims.

The T140D Special's swinging arm was revised to allow fitment of a wider a 4.25 x 18in Dunlop TT100 tyre. Stronger tubing was used and the rear brake caliper mounting switched to the top of the arm. Higher footrests (by 2in) and a revised centre stand allowed sufficient clearance for the silencer, although it still limited cornering angle on right-handers. A squared-off grab rail also replaced the small rack on the Specials.

Steering & front suspension

1976

The fork was unchanged, but adoption of a new single-rotor twistgrip meant a return to the in-line cable splitter box.

A knurled area provided on the handlebar for the brake master cylinder clamp caused the 'bar to receive a new part number.

Detail of side panel with 'limited edition' sticker which superseded original 'One of a Thousand' type.

Seat has red piping and 'Silver Jubilee' lettering on rear.

UK Jubilee has specially painted version of standard home-market fuel tank fitted to Bonnevilles from 1972 to 1981. This style is sometimes referred to as the 'breadbin'.

UK Jubilee model mudguard stripe continues to the edge on the front 'guard, but stops short on the rolled-edge rear 'guard.

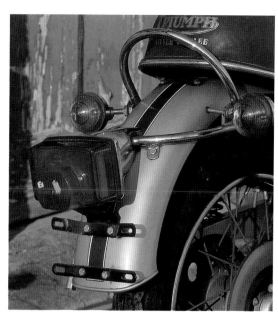

1977

Apart from the fitment of US-market chromed fork top shrouds on the Jubilee, no deviation was made from 1976 specification.

1978

A new and much more effective fork seal and retainer was the most significant update. The new parts carried the added benefit that they could be retro-fitted to any post-1970 model. UK and general export machines finally got the more glamorous chromed upper fork shrouds.

1979

Revised top and bottom yokes accommodated the repositioning of the steering lock and the placement of the new combined ignition switch and warning lamp panel. This was faced in black and housed main beam, neutral, indicator and oil warning lamps. The new panel nestled between the speedometer and tachometer at the front, before spreading out at the rear to allow the oil and main beam lights to flank the combined light and ignition switch. The D Special received new fork sliders with no provision for attaching the rearmost mudguard brace. On the handlebars, new Lucas switchgear proved much easier to operate. Finished in black, it incorporated the pivot points for the control levers, and the mounting for the front brake master cylinder.

Wheels, brakes & tyres

1976

Changes to the front of the machine were slight. A slightly thinner brake disc (the same thickness as fitted at the rear) was mounted on an unchanged front wheel. At the rear, the new disc with its underslung Lockheed caliper was the main update. A completely new wheel hub was introduced to carry the 10in cast-iron disc, which was operated by a re-sited brake pedal – pivoting on the right-hand rear engine plate – and a remote master cylinder under the seat.

1977

There were no changes to the T140V, but the Jubilee was clearly different in terms of finish. Instead of being in plain chrome, each wheel rim had a blue central band with white inner and red outer pinstriping, painted over the plating. The Jubilee's original tyres were a Dunlop K91, 4.10 x 19in at the front and 4.10 x 18in at the rear, with red lining and directional arrows on the sidewalls.

1978

The front wheel gained sealed bearings and the rear now had a new rim to suit the stouter 9-gauge spokes introduced following a spate of spoke breakages caused by the greater retarding power of the disc brake introduced for 1976.

1979

Revision of the wheels on the T140E models was limited to the polishing and lacquering of the hubs. On the D Special, however, the wheels were a real talking point, being US-made Lester seven-spoke alloy castings in the very latest style. With polished alloy outer rim and 'spoke' edges, they were otherwise all-black.

Front tyre size remained at 4.10 x 19in while the rear tyre initially grew to 4.25 x 18in. When problems arose of the rear tyre fouling the mudguard when a passenger was carried, it reverted to the old 4.10 x 18in size.

The 10in discs continued to be specified front and rear, although the rear caliper moved – on the Special only – to the top of the swinging arm.

Seat & bodywork

1976

The seat's base pan was revised, enabling both hinges to be standardised. Smoother material now covered the sides, while the wide rubber seat trim introduced in 1971 and abandoned after 1972 returned, now with a decorative chromed strip. A slight increase in the thickness of the padding enhanced comfort.

The chromed front mudguard no longer required holes for number plate attachment as front plates had ceased to be a legal requirement in the UK. The front guard also dispensed with its two front braces in favour of a bridge-brace of a type fitted on the T150 Trident, which was discontinued after 1974.

Some alteration of the chromed rear guard was needed to clear rear brake components. Fuel tank colours were the same as for 1974 and '75, and the different fuel tanks for the UK and US markets were unchanged.

1977

The Jubilee's seat was the first of a design which would (apart from the special colours) become standard on all Bonnevilles for the following year. The familiar aeration on the seat top was gone, replaced by a narrower cross-hatched panel. On the Jubilee the panel was covered in blue vinyl along with the rest of the seat. Red piping ran round the top perimeter of the rear portion before running downward along the sides and looping back up towards the front of the seat. The lower rubber trim was blue with the decorative chrome stripe. The Triumph logo was displayed in silver on the back of the unit.

Mudguards were painted rather than chromed on the Jubilee Bonnevilles, and followed the scheme on the wheel rims. A centre stripe of blue flanked by white inner and red outer pinstriping was applied over a base coat of silver.

For the first time, T140Vs were offered with a choice of colours. Tank graphics were unchanged, but Polychromatic Blue (called Pacific Blue in the USA) and White joined the previous year's scheme of Cherokee Red and White. Jubilee fuel tanks were the same as those specified for their respective market on the standard model, except for colour. While graphics retained the same layout, the blue and silver theme continued. A blue side panel was applied over a silver base in the UK, while the US version sported blue flashes – curved back in the usual fashion from the top of the tank badges – over a silver base. In all markets, the pinstriping was in white and red, with the red sandwiched between two white lines.

The side panels were all-new, like the seat and rear shocks, but with changes to finish they were destined to become standard items on all Bonneville models. They fitted over the existing panels and, on the Jubilee, they were plain silver with a special extended badge. The top of the badge was similar to the existing 'Bonneville' badges, but there was a triangular extension underneath the Bonneville name at the rear. This enclosed a Union Jack in the centre flanked by the words 'Silver Jubilee' and with either 'One of a Thousand' or 'Limited Edition' underneath. The panels themselves featured a new mounting system with a single screw just below the badge, backed up by a concealed spring attached to a metal-lined eyelet on the inside of each panel, running over the top of the carburettors and pulling the two panels together.

On the chainguard, the Jubilee theme continued in silver with a blue styling stripe along the upper part about ½in from the top edge. Tapering

D Special wears seven-spoke Lester cast wheels. Original US version had two-into-one exhaust system and a smaller fuel tank.

down to a point just before the rear end of the guard, the stripe was double-lined in white and red. The only other detail of finish to mark the Jubilee apart was its chrome-plated rear light housing, now painted black on standard models.

1978

For 1978, all Bonneville models were equipped with the Jubilee-type seat, but without the garish colours. A slight change to the cover saw the cross-ribbed top panel extend down on either side at the front following the piping as it dipped down where the rider's thigh rested. Two versions were available, a narrow-nosed one to suit the US fuel tank and a broader-nosed version for the wider UK tank. Seats were all-black or all-brown to complement the brown and gold paint option. All still carried the rubber trim with a chrome strip and bore the Triumph logo on the rear.

US machines retained their chrome mud-guards, but in the UK painted guards were sup-plied with T140V models. In all markets, the front mudguard fixing bolts were now provided with nylon washers to protect the finish on the guards. The home market choice of colours was Tawny Brown and Gold or Aquamarine and Silver. With

Tawny Brown, the front mudguard carried a curved band of Gold, lined with a brown inner and white outer stripe, across the mudguard mid-way between the central brace and the guard's leading edge. In the case of the other colour option, the base colour was Polychromatic Aqua-marine with a Silver stripe lined in black (inner) and gold (outer). At the rear, the styling band was positioned just below the lifting handle.

Petrol tanks retained the previous year's graph-ics, but in the new colours. For the UK, this meant a Tawny Brown or Aquamarine base colour with a Gold or Silver panel on the side. Pinstriping was double around the panels and executed in brown and white or black and gold respectively.

US machines were offered in the same Tawny Brown and Gold scheme, plus Astral Blue and Silver or Black and Candy Apple Red. In the first case, pinstriping was double and applied in brown and white, while the other schemes had lining in black and gold.

Side panels were now one-piece mouldings as fitted to the Jubilee, but gained an extra retaining spring linking them. T140V models for the UK had their side panels finished in the base colour matching that of their fuel tank, with a contrasting strip of the secondary colour running along the lower edge and all bar the last inch or two of the rear edge of the panel. This was separated with double pinstriping in the appropriate colours. In the USA, side panels were plain black. The 'Bonneville' badges remained, with gold lettering on a black ground in the 'States. In the UK, two different combinations were used on badges. Tawny Brown and Gold machines had black lettering on a silver ground, while the others had a gold-on-white scheme.

1979

A new seat with a more pronounced step was introduced on the D Special. Covered in black with a square, quilted pattern on the top, it retained the seat pan of the part it replaced. T140E models had a reworked version of the previous year's seat, now with a lock and covered in either black or brown depending on the paint finish. Chromed headlamp brackets matched the finish on the new headlamp shell.

Fuel tanks continued largely unchanged save for paintwork. The only other update was to UK and general export tanks, which finally lost their rubber knee-grips.

Choice of colour schemes for the prospective Bonneville owner was wider than ever in 1979. UK owners could choose from a Black tank with reshaped colour panels on the sides in Metallic Red, double-lined in gold, or a Beige tank having Metallic Gold sides with black inner and white outer pinstriping. The first scheme came with black side covers and seat, while the second one featured Beige side panels and a brown seat cover. New side panel badges included the figures '750' under the Bonneville name. Lettering was chrome on black on machines with black and red tanks, and black on chrome for the beige scheme.

US models kept the same tank graphics, but could be had in three colour combinations. A Dark Blue tank with Silver top colour flashes, lined in black inner and gold outer pinstripes was offered with Dark Blue side panels as the first option. US models also got the new-shape badges and, on this scheme, the lettering was chrome on a grey background. The other two choices were a Black tank with Silver flashes lined in black and gold, or a Candy Apple Red tank with Black flashes double-lined in gold. With both schemes, side panels were in plain black with badge lettering in chrome on a black background.

Both UK and US models wore the same chromed mudguards as in 1978.

The T140D was different again. Mudguards were still in chrome, but were much shorter – and less effective. The D Special was finished in Black with gold lining picking out the scallop shape of the US-market tank colour flashes, sandwiching

the plainer UK-style tank badge rather than the 'small eyebrow' type still fitted to other US machines. Side panels, too, were in Black with two parallel lines running horizontally under the badge. The badge itself was exclusive to the Special, with 'Special' in red under the 'Bonneville' name, which was chrome on a black ground.

Any model could now be ordered in any market. Growing numbers of US-specification Bonnevilles were appearing on British roads, and at the same time UK models were also seen in the USA, usually, although not always, without rubber fork gaiters.

Electrics

1976
The only recorded changes to the ignition and timing were the revision of the coil mounting brackets to accommodate the added rear brake master cylinder and reservoir.

T140D detail, showing right foot brake and brake light switch.

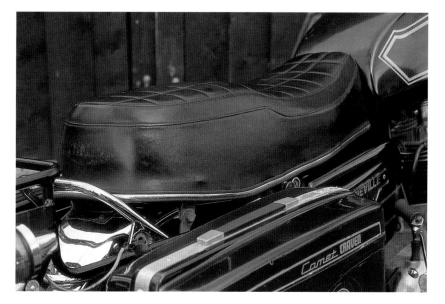

Seat with pronounced step, introduced on the T140D, was later adopted across the Bonneville range. Fuel tank's double 'thick and thin' gold lining is correct.

prices were increasingly uncompetitive with Japanese rivals. So it was no surprise that a Yuasa 12N9 4B1 battery replaced the costly Lucas PUZ5A unit for this model year.

1979

From the start of the 1979 season all Bonnevilles were equipped with Lucas Rita electronic ignition. This advance was made easier by the adoption of a negative-earth electrical system and a three-phase RM24 10.5-ampere alternator with its associated 3DS rectifier. A new ZD715 Zener diode attached to the aluminium air filter housing regulated alternator output.

The ignition system consisted of a sender unit housed in the former points compartment on the timing chest. This triggered a AB11 amplifier unit hidden behind the right side panel. Enclosing the magnetic pick-ups was a finned alloy cover which was polished on T140E models but black with polished sections on the D Special. Timing could be set by moving the back plate after slackening two clamping screws.

On the handlebars, new Lucas switchgear finished in black proved much easier to operate and incorporated the pivot points for slightly dog-legged alloy control levers, as well as the mounting for the front brake master cylinder on the right. Warning lamps now joined the combined lighting and ignition switch in a panel bolted to the top yoke between the instruments. Tail light and indicators were unchanged.

Instruments

1976

New faces without the 'NVT' (Norton Villiers Triumph) logo appeared on both speedometer and tachometer, although both of these instruments were otherwise unchanged.

1977

No changes were listed for the 1977 season.

1978

Most machines continued to carry the Smiths speedometer and tachometer. However, there were periods when the Smiths instruments were unavailable and French-made Veglia clocks were sourced to maintain production, only some of them displaying the Meriden logo on their faces. In the tachometer drive box, a revised washer helped reduce the incidence of drive failure.

1979

The Veglia instruments used sporadically in 1978 were now specified for all Bonneville models and mounted directly into a new binnacle shared with the warning lamps and ignition switch.

All switchgear was now labelled. The new left-side handlebar unit had cast-in function labels, but its right-side companion made do with cheap looking plastic stickers. Similar stickers were provided on the headlamp shell, indicating the function of each warning lamp and the positions of the ignition switch. The latter featured a more easily-used layout for the individual controls. At the rear of the machine, the indicators and stop and tail lamp lenses were revised.

1977

No changes were listed for the 1977 season.

1978

A Lucas 45/40W headlamp provided superior illumination, while at the rear the stop and tail light housing was no longer painted but polished and coated in clear lacquer. A louder Lucas 6H horn appeared initially, but Lucas were easing themselves out of the motorcycle business and their

Chapter 9

Even more new models: 1980-82

By 1980, Triumph's bubble seemed to have burst in the USA, with large numbers of unsold 1979 models left in showrooms and warehouses. The factory was forced to make drastic cuts in its sales forecasts for the 'States, with the result that more US-specification machines appeared on the home market. For the first time, the home market was officially deemed more significant than the USA, a sign that the old-fashioned 54bhp T140 twin was doomed as a contender in world markets.

Three new Bonnevilles for 1981 addressed dwindling sales. This initiative was not as rash as it might have seemed, since all of the 'new' models were based squarely on the existing T140. With

production at Meriden now undertaken in ever-smaller batches of machines, it was possible to offer an increasing number of colour and equipment options too. Anything, in fact, to sell a few more machines. The new variants were two versions of the Bonneville Executive, a tourer in both electric and kick-start versions equipped with fairing, top box and panniers, while the third was a machine intended for police evaluation. Coded T140AV, the police model featured 'Anti-Vibration' (AV) flexible engine mountings devised to make the Triumph competitive as a fleet choice against BMW's smooth boxer twin.

Continuing to search for different ways of

A definitive version of the late Bonneville – the US T140E of 1981. This example was bought and registered in the UK.

A 'smoke' paint finish helped make 1980s Meriden products look more modern. This US 1982 T140ES belongs to Bill Morrow, who is European sales manager at Performance Cycles, Shrewsbury, Massachusetts.

Limited edition machines became popular with major manufacturers around 1980. This 1982 T140LE Bonneville Royal is the UK version, with all engine castings coated in black.

serving up the same old dish, Triumph came up with another version of the Limited Edition theme, the T140LE Bonneville Royal, for 1982. The T140E and ES models continued to be available, as did the Executive, but the Royal – commemorating the wedding of Prince Charles to Lady Diana Spencer – was the only fresh model.

Mechanically no different from the ES, the LE was launched in July 1981, but was officially a 1982 model. Like the Jubilee model before it, each Royal came with a certificate of authenticity and three versions of the model eventually emerged. Two UK models, in standard and deluxe trim, were accompanied by a third variant for the USA.

Engine

1980

Although production started at engine number PB 25001, the main 1980 update was provision of an electric starter for the new T140ES model from engine number CB 29901. Prior to that, the only significant change was a four-valve oil pump designed to reduce wet-sumping, together with a revised timing cover to accommodate it. The new pump could be fitted to earlier engines provided the timing cover was machined or replaced with the modified version.

Fitting the electric starter called for more revision. The motor itself was a 12-volt Lucas M3 unit fitted behind the cylinder block in the same place as the pre-unit engine's magneto. New crankcase and timing cover castings were required and the starter was bolted to the inner face of an extension of the timing chest, cast integrally with the right-side crankcase half. A removable section of the outer cover provided access to mounting bolts for the motor, which drove the inlet camshaft via an extra idler pinion running in bushes in both the crankcase and the timing cover. A Borg-Warner sprag clutch was used and the final reduction ratio was 20:1.

Exhaust pipes were slightly revised, giving the unchanged silencers a more upswept appearance. Due to the fall in US sales, a large number of T140D Specials were released on the UK market, where they received either the original two-into-one system or the T140F twin-silencer system.

1981

Production for the 1981 season started from engine number KD 28001.

The location of the starter motor obstructed access to the TDC locating provision, so for 1981 this reverted to its former position at the front of the crankcase on the timing side. The crankshaft

Bing CV carburettors were specified for all US models from mid-1981 onwards in order to meet emissions legislation. Extended side panels conceal and protect the Bings' untidy and fragile external linkages.

Black engine, with fin edges polished back to bare alloy, helped to modernise the looks of the Royal.

Amal Concentric Mark II carburettors on T140E.

was modified with notches to suit the new location system and now ran in a heavy-duty, four-lipped roller bearing on the timing side. At the same time, the oil feed to the exhaust tappets was deleted, and cam followers and their guide blocks were now identical for both exhaust and inlet.

Push-over fitting for the exhaust pipes made its return too. The threaded exhaust ports introduced for the T140D were retained, but now a stub fitting for the pipes was screwed in and a finned clamp held the pipes on. In the USA, unsold T140D models were offered with optional shorter, slash-cut, megaphone-style silencers in an effort to make them more appealing. While attending to the cylinder head, Meriden engineers also added oil seals to the inlet valve guides.

Machines with Anti-Vibration frames had a modified crankcase for the revised engine mounts and the crankshafts were re-balanced to a factor of 55 per cent.

1982
The only changes to the Bonneville engine for 1982 were cosmetic and confined to the T140LE Royal. Both UK versions had all-over black-painted engines, with just the edges of the cylinder and ignition pick-up cover fins being left unpainted and polished. Those LEs that reached the USA had unpainted crankcases polished in the normal fashion.

Fuel system & carburettors
1980
New fuel taps were fitted to cure leaking.

1981
Increasingly stringent US emission laws had made a move away from Amal MkII Concentric carburettors inevitable and this happened in 1981. While early E and ES models were shipped with revised MkII instruments with cable-operated chokes and larger-needle jets, these were replaced on later US machines by German Bing 32mm Type 94 constant-vacuum carburettors. In the UK, Amal MkII carburettors remained standard equipment on all but Executive models.

1982
The UK E and ES models continued to have MkII Concentrics, while Executives, Royals and all US exports breathed through Bings.

Transmission
1980
A revision to the primary chain tensioner meant that the chain could now be adjusted without draining the transmission oil.

1981

Changes were limited to fine-tuning of the clutch. All its plates were slightly thinner, allowing a cork rear face to be applied to the clutch housing. Also, the number of friction plates was reduced from seven to six and lighter T120-type clutch springs were fitted.

1982

There were no changes for 1982.

Frame & rear suspension

1980

From the start of 1980 production, Bonneville frames carried provision for the starter solenoid. The electric starter also called for a larger and more powerful Yuasa YB14 L battery, which made its appearance towards the end of the sales season. This meant a larger battery carrier and a recess in the seat pan to clear it. A bigger tool tray was incorporated at the same time.

A new swinging arm eased production by employing identical left- and right-hand legs, and tube outside diameter was increased from 32mm to 38mm. T140E and ES models now fell in line with the Special by featuring the same raised footrests, centre stand mounting and rear brake caliper location. The upswept silencers required new mounting brackets further up the frame, while the remote fluid reservoir for the rear brake moved to a position directly on top of the master cylinder casting. Pillion footrest mounts were also relocated to suit the higher silencer position.

1981

Although Girling rear shock absorbers were still fitted in 1981, the company had warned that they would not be available for much longer. Triumph had ceased to be a volume component purchaser and specialist suppliers were looking to more profitable markets than motorcycles.

Although some Executives were available in 1980, this was classed as a 1981 model and there was no model identification in the frame number, which carried either a T140E or ES prefix. The Anti-Vibration frames had rubber-bushed engine mountings added and their serial numbers had an AV suffix.

1982

Marzocchi rear shock absorbers began to be fitted as supplies of Girlings ran out. US machines were the first to receive the new units, which eventually became standard on all Bonnevilles. Other than that, the only changes were to colours. Standard Royal models on sale in the UK got grey springs on their shock absorbers to match the grey-painted frame and centre stand. US buyers

got more traditional black frames, as did owners of the UK deluxe LE models.

Steering & front suspension

1980

The front fork and steering remained unchanged for 1980, although a number of E and ES models were assembled using US-specification parts and marketed in the UK as the 'Bonneville American'. They differed from true export machines in carrying the fork gaiters normal on UK models.

1981

All models now had a groove machined in the top of each fork slider to accept a circlip to retain the fork seal. Executives were made available with twin front discs later in the year, for which a new right-side fork slider casting was necessary.

1982

UK forks for 1982 had their sliders painted black but were otherwise unchanged, save for the option of twin Lockheed front discs, as fitted to Executive models, for which a revised right-side slider

Fork sliders had polished finish in 1981; on most later machines they are black.

Switchgear adopted from 1979 was more user-friendly.

was specified and soon fitted to all Bonnevilles whether or not twin discs were fitted. Royals also had black sliders except for the deluxe, which sported a polished alloy finish.

All headlamp brackets were now rubber-mounted, while US machines received lower 6½in-rise bars in line with UK machines, leaving only the UK-market 'Electro USA' model with the 8½in-rise US style.

Wheels, brakes & tyres

1980
The front brake master cylinder was now of semi-opaque plastic, allowing visual checking of the fluid level without removing the cap. The rear wheel received a new hub to allow the speedometer drive to be switched from the right to the left of the hub. To facilitate this, a thinner disc brake rotor with the necessary shorter bolts was also fitted. As mentioned above, the rear brake master cylinder now carried its fluid reservoir on top and both were re-sited under the right-hand side panel, while the brake pedal was strengthened. Avon Roadrunner tyres replaced the Dunlops fitted as original equipment for so many years.

1981
Morris alloy wheels became an option later in the year, replacing the Lesters, and could be specified for any Bonneville. As mentioned above, twin-disc front brakes became available late in the season, initially on Executives. The new wheels

were again finished in black, but were plainer with a raised rib in the centre of each of the seven spokes. Like the Lester wheels, they had polished rims and the edges of the ribs on the spokes were also bright. Later in the model year, single-disc rotors lost their chrome plating and a more effective Dunlopad friction material was specified.

1982
Morris cast wheels, already available as an option, became standard equipment on ES models, now known as Electros. Lockheed alloy brake calipers were now specified across the Bonneville range, with smaller-diameter 9.8in disc rotors. Twin front discs, standard for the Executive, were an option on all models. Sintered Dunlopad pads became standard equipment.

In the UK, the rear sprocket shed two teeth to give the engine an easier time and, because of this, the chain was shortened from 107 to 106 links. US machines continued with a 47-tooth sprocket.

The T140LEs featured the same cast alloy Morris wheels and twin front discs as the Electros, except for the deluxe, which, perversely, had a single disc on its spoked front wheel. Traditional spoked wheels with chromed rims could be specified by US purchasers if preferred.

Seat & bodywork

1980
Apart from a cut-out in the seat pan to accommodate the ES model's larger battery, the seat

Rear brake caliper arrangement for 1981 (right), with assembly now placed above swinging arm. Tidy rear parcel rack (far right) was standard on T140E from 1979.

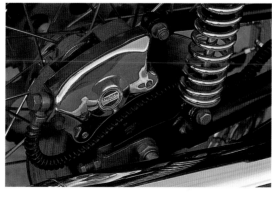 

options were much as before. One small revision was the absence of the restraining wire that stopped the seat opening too far, replaced by positive stops on the hinges. All 1980 seats were finished in black, with UK machines retaining the 'flatter' 1979-pattern seats (even in the case of the home-market T140E/ES American), while machines shipped across the Atlantic got the stepped T140D Special type.

Side panels were also all in black regardless of model, although the D models continued with their twin gold stripes. Side panel badges were also unchanged except that colours were standardised as chrome lettering on a black ground for all. The right side panel now featured a small window near its lower edge to allow inspection of the rear brake's fluid level. Mudguards were the same chromed items as previously, with the D models keeping their truncated versions.

The fuel tanks only altered in terms of finish, although T140Ds sold on the home market had the option of a larger UK tank finished in black with two horizontal gold lines mirroring those on the side panels. Tank graphics on other models for both the home and US markets stayed the same, although there were new colour options for all.

Two options were listed for the UK. Steel Grey with a Candy Apple Red panel, double-lined in heavy black, was the alternative to a plain black tank with just the outline of the secondary panel traced with broad inner and thin outer white pinstripes. US riders were offered a choice of three colour schemes, all featuring the curved upper and lower 'scallop' colour flashes. Colours, all with the flashes lined in gold, were Black with Candy Apple Red, Grey with Black, and Olympic Flame with Black. UK models, including the E and ES American, wore the plain Triumph name badges, as did the T140D Special, while US machines still had the 'eyebrow' type.

1981

The seat situation got more complex with the introduction of the Executive models. Most E and ES models came equipped with the stepped type introduced on the T140D Special, covered in black with the chrome and black lower trim strip, although the earlier, flatter item generally used on kick-start models was also available. Each seat came in two versions to suit either US or UK fuel tanks. Additionally, US-market Executives had a stepped 'King & Queen' seat with a raised pillion section and a distinctive lip at the rear of the rider's portion.

Mudguards changed from chromed to polished stainless steel across the Bonneville model range, with the exception of the Executive which reverted to painted guards complementing the smoked tank finish. The new front guards were

similar to the ones they replaced, retaining the U-shaped central mounting bracket and rear brace.

During the course of the 1981 sales season, the supply of traditional British-made tanks dwindled. Old-style tanks were still fitted to E and ES models and early UK-market Executives, but it was not long before Executives were supplied with a new Italian-sourced tank. This retained the central mounting as before, but featured a flip-up filler cap and the plain Triumph name badges already used on UK and 'Rest-of-World' tanks. The new tank was of the same 4½-gallon (Imperial measure) capacity, but differently shaped from traditional Triumph designs.

Colour choices were expanded as the factory sought to woo every possible taste. US tanks kept the 'eyebrow' tank badge, in chrome with the centre of the lettering in black, for a final year, and locking filler caps were also specified. US tanks came in a choice of six colours, although in reality only the two smoked paint schemes actually crossed the Atlantic. Both lined in gold, they were Smoked Astral Blue with a Silver scallop above the tank badge only, or Smoked Olympic Flame with an Ivory scallop. Both of these schemes also featured side panels coloured to match the tank's main colour. The main colour predominated at the front of the panel, fading into smoke towards the rear. Later in the year, reshaped side panels were fitted to enclose the bulky and unsightly Bing carburettors. These panels were divided diagonally from front to rear, with the upper portion bright and the lower heavily smoked, separated by a gold pinstripe.

Four other US paint schemes listed were available in the UK and Europe as 'Bonneville American' models. Three of these featured both upper and lower colour scallops on the tanks, and all side panels in black with 'Bonneville 750' badges in chrome on black. ES models also wore an 'Electro' sticker on the side panel, with the 'o' struck through with a lightning bolt. All lined in gold, the colours available were Steel Grey with Black, Black with Candy Apple Red, and Silver Blue with Black. Another option was an all-Black finish with just the outline of the scallops picked out in gold.

UK tanks could be ordered in a choice of six colour schemes too. Four followed the established graphics, with a base colour overlaid with a contrasting side-colour panel. Schemes available were: Black with Candy Apple Red, twin-lined gold; Steel Grey with Candy Apple Red, twin-lined black; Silver Blue with Black, twin-lined gold (inner) and black (outer); and all-Black with twin gold lines outlining the shape of the panel. Tank badges were white in-filled letters on a black ground except on the Black version, which had black in-filled letters on a black ground. Side

By 1981, virtually any combination of machine specification could be purchased in home or export markets. This is a 1981 US T140E.

panels for all these were in black with chrome-on-black badges and the 'Electro' sticker if applicable.

Two other options were listed, featuring smoked paintwork and matching side panels. Colours were Smokey Blue or Smokey Flame, with a single gold line running around the lower front corner of the tank. Badges were black on a chrome ground.

The T140 Executive could be specified in E or ES versions. US models, which arrived later in the season, were the ES type with the new fuel tank. The principal difference between the Executive and standard E and ES models was the fork-mounted cockpit fairing and matching hard luggage. First released in the UK, early Executives sported the standard UK-type E model seat and tank, and were offered in either Smokey Red or Smokey Blue colour schemes. In both cases, the tank had a single gold pinstripe around the lower front quarter.

Later models were equipped with Italian-made fuel tanks and a two-level seat with all-black lower trim could be specified. On these tanks the gold pinstripe extended right round at the front to enclose the tank badge.

The fairing interior had a 'leather-look' plastic finish and two round black mirrors were mounted

on the side bulges of the fairing. Initially, a clear screen was fitted, but later models got a tinted screen with a black trim along its upper edge.

The quickly detachable panniers and top box were finished in the same colours as the tank and fairing, while the side panels were divided diagonally like the US E and ES variants, which also featured the extended panels, with their single Allen screw fastening, covering their Bing carburettors. The smoked finish generally got darker towards the rear of any panel it was applied to, but no two finishes were exactly the same due to the fact that all were hand-sprayed. Tank badges were the standard UK-market Triumph name type and slightly smaller versions of these were also used at the rear of the panniers until a simpler, round badge – also bearing the Triumph name – replaced them later in the year.

1982

It is easiest to list the changes to the seat and bodywork of the 1982 range by model, as this was the main area of change for the year. Obviously the Royal was the most radically different, but the introduction of new components from new suppliers meant changes across the range.

For the T140LE Royal, two levels of finish

were available on UK and 'Rest-of-World' Royals, and a third for the USA. It seems likely that the deluxe UK variant was originally intended for the 'States, but in the event fewer than 50 of the T140LE Royal models made it across the Atlantic and all were of the more sober, later US version.

A new dual seat in black vinyl was fitted to the more subdued standard model intended as the UK version of the T140LE Royal. This had a less pronounced step between pillion and rider's portion of the seat, and the quilted panel on the top surface was wider than on earlier seats. The stepped seat from the Executive model was used on the deluxe Royal, re-covered and now featuring a light grey top panel with a black strip between rider and pillion, and black sides.

Fuel tanks on all T140LE models were the new, Italian-made 4-gallon units, or the smaller US version on the deluxe. UK tanks were chromium-plated with either black or Smokey Blue (on the deluxe) stylised flashes top and bottom of each side, separated by a gold-on-black Triumph logo and lined in gold. On both versions, a plastic 'Royal Wedding' badge plugged the tank mount-

ing hole, but the deluxe version got the benefit of the small 'eyebrow' tank badges. The few Royals exported to the USA benefited from more subtle all-black tanks double-lined in gold around the edges of their sides.

Side panels were the extended type to protect the Bing carburettors and were either black or Smokey Blue, matching the finish of the tank, with a single, diagonal gold pinstripe curving down from top left to bottom right under a new badge created specially for the T140LE. These carried a second deck of lettering below the familiar Bonneville name, which bore the word 'Royal' in gold and a small chromed crown after it on a black background. Deluxes had the same badge but with the lettering in blue on a silver ground. US machines had black side panels with chrome on black lettering. On all versions, a gold 'Limited Edition' transfer appeared in the lower left corner of each side panel.

Mudguards remained stainless steel, while the other pressed steel was the same as the rest of the range apart from the deluxe having chrome on the headlamp brackets, fork top shrouds, side stand,

The 1982 T140ES has a fuel tank that Meriden sourced from Italy. Tilted front indicator should be level, like rear one.

Flatter seat, German-made rectangular indicators and black fork sliders are all features of the 1982 T140ES.

sparking plug caps, rear brake pedal, instrument cups and indicator stems.

The seat on Executive models remained either the stepped type or the T140E pattern from the previous year. An alternative fairing developed for police use was offered for 1982. Offering much more protection than the original Executive fairing, it featured a higher screen and detachable lower panels to protect the rider's legs. Mudguards were painted to match the overall colour scheme, and for 1982 Executive options were Smokey Flame or Black. In the case of the Black scheme, the fuel tank was double-lined in gold with a thicker outer line, and the fairing and luggage were lined to match. Tank and side panel badges featured gold lettering on a black ground.

Changes to the T140E and ES models were few. Seat options remained as in the previous year and the principal changes were to the colour schemes offered. Seat finish for both the UK and US markets was standardised with a black quilted seat cover, enlivened by a chrome lower trim. By now all fuel tanks fitted at the factory were the squarer, Italian-made items either in the 4-gallon (UK) or 3.6-gallon (US) capacities.

Colour schemes were reduced from the previous year and in the UK only three variations were

listed. The first was plain black with a single gold pinstripe around the side of the fuel tank, and black side panels with silver-on-black lettered badges. The other two were Smokey Flame or Smokey Blue paired with Gold. Both options featured a similar gold pinstripe around the side of the tank, while the side panels were finished in the smoked colour. Badges on the side panels sported chrome lettering on a black ground regardless of overall colour scheme.

For the USA, four colour schemes were offered. Two featured smoked finishes and had curved styling flashes above the Triumph name badge only. These were the same colours used for UK machines, but the Smokey Flame was teamed with Ivory in the USA while the Smokey Blue was paired with Silver. Both had side panels in the

A 1982 UK Bonneville Royal. Marzocchi Strada rear suspension units with remote reservoirs were also fitted to the following year's eight-valve TSS. Detail shot shows Limited Edition plate on the Royal's headstock.

Side panel contrasts. US electric-start model (top) has plain black lower section, whereas UK Royal (above) has glossy upper half and matt lower part.

main smoked colour with chrome-on-black lettering. An 'Electro' transfer in gold on each side panel announced the presence of a starter motor.

The other two colour options for the US were Silver Blue and Black or Black and Candy Apple Red. In both cases, the tanks bore contrasting styling flashes both above and below the tank badge in the second colour. Both schemes featured black side panels with chrome-on-black badges, while the mudguards were polished stainless steel as on all T140E and ES models.

Electrics
1980
Uprating of the Lucas Rita electronic ignition introduced the previous year was achieved by

Tank contrasts. Simple but effective graphics on 1981 US T140E (top). Paint scheme described as Smoked Flame/Misty Red (centre) may have been inspired by similar finishes seen on BMW tourers from the mid-1970s. Italian-made Royal tank (bottom) was chromed before painting.

Extended timing cover envelopes the T140ES starter motor. Electronic ignition trigger is under finned cover.

using higher-output trigger coils at the ignition sensors. Together with internal revisions to the AB11 amplifier unit, this produced a stronger spark at low revs, making electric starting easier.

Most of the electrical changes resulted from the introduction on the T140ES of electric start, as described in the engine section. These models were equipped with a higher-output 14 amp Lucas RM24 three-phase alternator, a Yuasa YB14L battery and a new triple Zener diode pack dealing separately with each output phase of the alternator and mounted directly to the alloy air filter housing. A starter solenoid was concealed under the right side panel and the starter switch incorporated in the right-hand handlebar cluster. Indicators were, at long last, rubber-mounted to combat damage inflicted by vibration.

1981

At the start of the year, there were no changes to the Bonneville's electrical system, which continued with the battery and alternator specifications to suit either electric or kick-start machines. From mid-season, however, only the higher-output ES-type alternator was fitted, regardless of whether or not the machine had electric start, so only the battery size varied between E and ES.

Indicators also changed during the year. As supplies of chromed Lucas indicators had dried up, rectangular German-made units in black plastic on painted metal stems replaced them. The orange lenses carried moulded-in Triumph logos.

1982

The only improvements for 1982 were the introduction of a more powerful 60/45W sealed-beam headlamp unit and sturdier indicators.

Instruments

1980

By 1980, Smiths instruments were no longer available, so only Veglia speedometers and tachometers were now used.

1981

There were no changes for 1981.

1982

There were no changes for 1982.

French-made Veglia instruments started replacing Smiths components from 1978 and were the usual wear by 1981.

Chapter 10

Meriden's final products: 1983

Time would prove that 1983 was to be the last year of Bonneville production at Meriden, but at the start of the year optimists saw two new models as possible saviours for the troubled factory. For 1983, the T140E and ES models continued, as did the Executive, but the new custom-style TSX and the eight-valve T140W TSS were the machines on which Triumph's hopes rested.

With cash flow causing ever-increasing problems and the ailing company's credit rating at an

Believed to be the last Bonneville to leave the Meriden factory, this 1983 US-market T140E was registered in the UK.

all-time low, the machines that actually left the factory often differed from published specifications. It was often a case of fitting whatever was to hand in order to get a few machines out and a few pounds in. Mechanically, the TSX was identical to the T140ES with the exception of its large-bore exhaust system, but the TSS was a very different story. With a top speed of 125mph or better, the TSS was a move in the right direction, but unfortunately poor build quality and lack of development let it down.

Engine

Sadly the eight-valve T140W TSS engine was a case of too little, too late. By 1983, cash-starved Triumph could not afford the necessary extensive development of the new engine designed to put the performance back into the Bonneville.

Since the late 1960s, famed engine specialist Weslake had been offering an eight-valve top-end conversion for the bigger Triumph twins. Noting the power increase offered by this conversion,

Distinctively 'custom' look for TSX, with 16in rear wheel and fat tyre, high handlebars, electric start and Yamaha-like styling decals.

Redesigned cylinder head makes eight-valve T140W TSS easily recognisable. This original example owned by Middlesex rider Bob Nicholson has covered only 11,000 miles.

Meriden engineers developed an in-house version with technical help and marketing rights obtained from Weslake. Eventually unveiled in the form of the TSS, the new machine produced a respectable 59bhp, but suffered from porous cylinder head castings and other avoidable faults, which resulted in a spate of warranty claims that a beleaguered factory could ill-afford.

Standard T140 crankcases and gearbox castings were employed on the TSS, but with higher-specification roller main bearings. A sturdy new crankshaft was at the heart of the new model: designed to cope with 10,000rpm engine speeds, the one-piece forged shaft had larger-diameter (1.875in) big-end journals and thicker webs. A completely new cylinder block had its bores spaced ½in further apart than the rest of the range, requiring the new connecting rods to run slightly offset on the gudgeon pins at the small ends.

Squarer in shape and more closely finned than the standard T140 block, the new block was finished in black with the edges of the fins polished. Flat-topped 9.5:1 pistons – with four pockets machined to allow sufficient clearance for the valves – ran in steel liners.

Finning on the black one-piece cylinder head and rocker box matched the cylinder block, while the TSS dispensed with a traditional head gasket in favour of two separate Cross-ring seals seated in the head. Following T140 practice, ten bolts held the head down, but the four outer bolts ran straight through the cylinder casting and threaded into the crankcase. The new head casting also provided for bolt-on flange fixing of the exhaust pipes, each of which had a sealing ring at its port to ensure a gas-tight fit.

Smaller valves (for which the sizes were listed

TSS used existing T140ES crankcase castings, but one-piece rocker covers are a feature of the eight-valve head. Side panels are finished in half-and-half matt and gloss black.

Engine outer covers are polished on the TSX, with rest of power unit in black except for bare-metal fin edges.

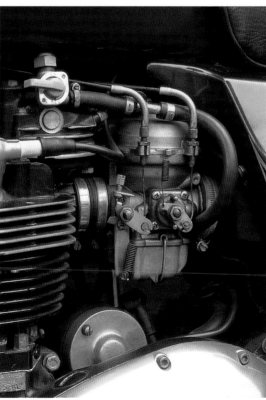

On the TSX, the Bing carburettors are not covered by extended side panels.

in a curious mix of metric and Imperial measurements) had diameters of 1.148-1.152in (inlet) and 0.990-0.995in (exhaust). They were inclined at a steepened 30-degree angle and surrounded a central 10mm sparking plug. The rocker box had two separate covers running almost the full width of the cylinder head, giving access to the forked rockers, each of which controlled a pair of valves. Allen bolts secured the covers and modified T140 pushrods in tubes activated special cams – mild inlet, fierce exhaust – specified for the TSS.

Finish was all-black apart from the edges of the cylinder and head fins, and polished alloy on the primary drive, timing and gearbox covers.

As for the regular Bonneville engine, unsurprisingly there was little change for 1983. A stronger intermediate timing wheel was fitted to electric-start machines, and the TSX engine had rocker boxes and cylinder heads finished in black with the edges of the fins in polished alloy. After engine number 33965, TSX engines also ran 7.4:1 pistons instead of the 7.9:1 versions specified for the rest of the range, except for the TSS.

The TSX exhaust was a one-off. Dispensing with a balance pipe, the 1¾in downpipes featured towards their bottom bend flat chrome strips, which attached to the engine for support. A balance pipe running under the frame linked short, well-baffled, megaphone-type silencers.

Fuel system & carburettors

UK Bonnevilles continued with 30mm Amal Concentric MkII carburettors, while US models kept the 32mm Bing instrument. TSS models sold in the UK benefited from larger 34mm Concentrics but US buyers of the eight-valver had to be content with the smaller Bing CVs, because of emission legislation.

Transmission

Gearbox modifications were limited to a revision of the mainshaft thread from engine number DEA 33133. The thread was changed from ⅝in to ⅝in, and necessitated a new lock washer and self-locking nut. Slight revision of gear ratios on the TSS gave higher overall gearing to suit the extra power, while the cruiser-style TSX rear sprocket went up to 47 teeth, to perk up acceleration and compensate for a change of rear wheel size.

Frame & rear suspension

Frames were unaltered across the range except on the TSS, which had a Brembo rear brake master cylinder and a revised swinging arm to accommodate the fatter rear tyre. Rear suspension units on the TSX were by Paioli and featured chromed

springs with black bodies, while US-market T140s got slimmer struts of the same make. For the rest of the range, Marzocchi units were retained: UK and 'Rest-of-World' T140 models kept Euro '74 items, while the TSS had more up-market Marzocchi Strada units with remote-damping oil reservoirs.

Steering & front suspension

UK models had by now dispensed with flexible fork gaiters. Otherwise the only change was on the TSX, which featured polished yokes and sliders to complement its custom cruiser image. The rest of the range had plain black sliders and yokes in the UK, although US machines' fork sliders were polished. The TSX had 8in-rise handlebars, while T140E and ES Bonnevilles continued with either slightly lower US-pattern 'bars or the flatter European type. All handlebars carried Magura alloy dog-leg control levers.

Wheels, brakes & tyres

Morris alloy wheels were fitted to all models except US T140s, which retained spoked wheels. Twin front disc brakes continued as an option, but the TSS had them as standard.

Marzocchi shock absorbers and single-disc rear brake on TSS (above left). Morris wheels, double discs and slim stainless steel front guard (above) lend a purposeful look to the front end of the TSS.

Magura levers, Doherty hand grips and Bumm rear-view mirrors were all on this TSS from new.

By 1983, T140E (above) has Marzocchi rear shock absorbers and, on this US example, polished front fork sliders.

Black and Candy Apple Red paint scheme (right) was applied to both US and UK T140E in 1983. TSX side panels (far right) carry styling stickers that were notoriously difficult to apply.

To achieve its distinctive look, the TSX's Morris rear wheel was of only 16in diameter and wore a wide 5.10-section tyre. On the 19in front wheel was a relatively skinny 3.25-section tyre in place of the usual 4.10 section. A Brembo rear brake caliper was fitted on the TSX, rather than the Lockheed unit used on the rest of the range.

Seat & bodywork

A completely new stepped seat, covered in broadly-ribbed black vinyl, appeared on the TSX, while the rest of the range continued with E and ES versions of the stepped and bench-style seats, plus the 'King and Queen' option on the Executive. The Euro-style fuel tank remained in use throughout 1983, although the TSX used a re-introduced 3.6-gallon (US) 'peanut' tank. It now featured a central hinged filler cap and had only one fuel tap, with a balance pipe linking it to a second fuel outlet on the other side of the tank. For the USA, a lockable tank filler was standard, but optional elsewhere.

Influenced by a new breed of custom-style catalogue machines selling in America, the TSX

broke new ground for Triumph in carrying vinyl stickers to provide colour contrast on the fuel tank and side panels. The bright red, orange and yellow (listing the colours from front to back) stickers were apparently a nightmare to apply without creasing due to the fact that they were placed on a double curvature. On the tank the stickers ran almost vertically up through the Triumph name badge on the side of the tank, before sweeping

Final form of seat, indicators and grab rail on T140E (above left). This style of grab rail and seat (above) are unique to the TSX, which also has short Paioli rear shock absorbers.

A finer point of originality: German-made rectangular indicator lens should have moulded-on Triumph logo.

Morris alloy wheels and single front disc brake were standard on the TSX (opposite). This particular machine was dealer-converted to left-foot brake operation when new.

back along the top and ending in a point on either side just before they reached the nose of the seat.

Traditional hand-applied gold pinstriping surrounded each sticker, with a double line along its leading and top edges. The treatment was repeated on the side panels, with near-horizontal stripes following the line of the moulding as it tipped in towards the underside of the seat. A TSX badge in chrome-outlined lettering on a black ground adorned the front of the inward-sloping upper face of each panel.

A choice of Black or Burgundy base colour was offered to the prospective TSX owner in the UK, and this extended to both mudguards, which were shorter than their counterparts on the rest of the range. On both colour options, the mudguards were lined in orange around their outer edges. A new chrome grab rail angled sharply up behind the rear of the seat. A modified version of the standard chainguard, which allowed the wider tyre to fit without fouling, was finished in chrome.

Bodywork across the rest of the range changed little for 1983, although by then almost any finish was available to get a machine built and paid for. Official UK colours for the T140E and ES were the previous year's Black and Candy Apple Red scheme, or a choice of Black or Burgundy, double-lined in gold on the fuel tank, with black side panels. Chrome-on-black lettering was the norm for tank badges except in the case of tanks with gold lining, which had lettering filled in with gold. US T140ES models with the Candy Apple Red and Black paintwork had tank styling flashes picked out in the secondary colour, like the 1979 T140D, while UK machines had these filled in with colour. Another option listed for the US was the Black with gold lining as available on the home market.

Fuel tanks on the UK TSS were black and double-lined in gold, while side panels were also black with a single gold line highlighting the moulding's shape. Press-on badges on the two-tone matt and gloss side panels proclaimed 'TSS' in gold on black. Tank badges had chrome lettering, in-filled with gold, on a black ground. In the US, the Black and Candy Apple Red scheme, with a flat-topped styling scallop on the tank, was apparently the most common finish on the TSS.

Bonneville Executives retained the smoked paint schemes both at home and in the USA. With the exception of the Executive and TSX models, mudguards were still in stainless steel.

Electrics

Ignition on the TSS was by a revised Lucas Rita electronic unit which gave 30 degrees of advance rather than the 38 degrees of the T140 unit.

Black headlamp brackets and shells continued for 1983 except on the TSX, which featured a chromed shell and a return to chromed wire headlamp brackets, this time attached to the front of both fork yokes. In addition, the upper fork shrouds on the TSX were also chromed, and the cruiser-style model reverted to the earlier-type Lucas chrome indicators too. The only other electrical change was fitment of a triple Zener diode pack on the TSS.

Veglia clocks and round Lucas indicators, as seen on a TSX.

Instruments

Because of its changed rear wheel and tyre sizes the TSX needed a revised ratio in its speedometer drive gearbox.

THE END OF A LEGEND – ALMOST

Although 1983 saw the last Bonneville leave the Meriden works, it was not quite the end of the story, even though Triumph Motorcycles (Meriden) Ltd went into voluntary liquidation on 26 August that year. Housebuilding magnate and Triumph enthusiast John Bloor moved in to buy the name, manufacturing rights, patents and trademarks. Much of the manufacturing plant and remaining parts stocks were acquired by Les Harris, who was already in business as a pattern parts specialist.

Harris obtained agreement from Bloor to make complete T140s under a licence agreement. After solving problems of component supply, mainly by procuring cycle parts from outside Britain, his company – L. F. Harris (Rushden) Ltd – resumed production of the Bonneville in slightly modified form

at its premises in Newton Abbot, Devon, on 25 June 1985.

Harris's efforts produced 1255 motorcycles, a phenomenal achievement for a tiny operation that gave many owners the pleasure of owning a brand new Bonneville. Production finally ceased at Newton Abbot in March 1988 when the licence agreement expired.

With so many T120 and T140 machines from 1959 to 1988 now restored, or being restored, to highly original condition, the Bonneville legend lives on into the new century. Of course, new Bonneville models will come from Bloor's thriving Hinckley-based Triumph Motorcycles Limited, where production of modern machines started up in 1991. For many classic Triumph fans, though, the only 'real' Bonnevilles were those made at Meriden.

Brochure shot of the Bonneville made by L. F. Harris under a licensing agreement with John Bloor in Devon from 1985 to 1988. It was not exported to the USA.

Chapter 11

Identification, Dating & Colours

Triumphs built at Meriden followed the generally adopted rule of motorcycle dating, whereby the age of the machine is determined by the frame number. However, as all Bonnevilles were given matching engine and frame numbers, the engine number should also correspond to the stated year of manufacture. The factory adopted this practice in 1956 and continued with it right up to the end of production in 1983.

A Bonneville's frame number is found on the frame downtube, on the left just beneath the steering head. There is a prefix, then the actual number, and then a suffix indicating the model. The first Bonnevilles had six-figure frame and engine numbers, but, from mid-season in 1960, 1960-62 duplex-framed models carry a D prefix to the number, starting at 101. With the arrival of unit construction in 1963, the prefix was changed to DU and the number sequence restarted at 101.

This practice continued until the 1969 season, when a new system of codes for the number prefixes indicated both the month and model year of an individual machine, as itemised in the accompanying table. It must be remembered that, certainly until the late 1970s, the nominal model year started from the end of August in the previous year, when the factory resumed production after the summer break.

The engine number is found on a pad on the crankcase, situated on the side below the base of

the cylinder block. Engine numbers follow the same practice as the frame numbers in that the number has a prefix and is followed by the appropriate suffix to denote the model.

Not surprisingly, over the years some machines have had engine changes or crankcase castings replaced. In some cases, twin-carburettor Bonneville engines or top ends may have been installed in other machines from Triumph's range, such as the 6T Thunderbird or TR6 Trophy.

MODEL DESIGNATION SUFFIX LETTERS

Letter	Model description	Period
No letter	UK model, road	1959
A	US model, road	1960 only
B	US model, street scrambler	1960 only
R	US model, road	After 1960
C	US model, street scrambler	After 1960
TT	US TT Specials	Mid-1966 to end of 1967
RT	US-only 750cc version	1970 only
V	Five-speed gearbox	After 1973
E	Emission-controlled model	After 1978
ES	Electric start	After 1980
D	Special	1979-80 only
LE	Limited Edition, Royal	1982 only
TSS	Eight-valve head	1983 only
TSX	Custom style model	After 1983
AV	Anti-vibration police frame	After 1981

DATE CODES (1969-80)

First letter	Build month
A	January
B	February
C	March
D	April
E	May
G	June
H	July
J	August
K	September
N	October
P	November
X	December

Second letter	Model year
C	1969
D	1970
E	1971
G	1972
H	1973
J	1974
K	1975
N	1976
P	1977
X	1978
A	1979
B	1980

DATE CODES (1981-83)

Letters	Model year
KDA	1981
EDA	1982
BEA	1983

PRINCIPAL YEAR-BY-YEAR CHANGES

1959
First year of production. Separate engine and gearbox. Magneto ignition with manual advance, 'chopped' Amal Monobloc carburettors, remote float bowl. Single downtube frame, valanced mudguards, enclosed headlamp nacelle. Dry-sump lubrication with separate oil tank on right. Seat black with grey trim.

1960
Duplex frame, separate chromed headlamp shell. Flexible fork gaiters. Crank-mounted alternator, magneto ignition with auto advance. Float chamber suspended from cylinder head steady. High-pipe competition variant launched in USA. Black seat, white piping.

1961
Lower tank rail added to duplex frame. Standard Monobloc carburettors. Anti-vibration brackets for oil tank and fuel tank with revised three-point mounting. Fully-floating brake shoes front and rear. Rear wheel now 18in diameter.

1962
Smiths Chronometric 140mph speedo replaces 120mph item. Two-tone grey/black seat with white piping.

1963
Unit-construction engine with nine-stud head. Coil ignition, points in timing cover. Frame reverts to single downtube. Front wheel changed from 19in to 18in.

1964
TT Special model for US market. External fork springs. Smiths magnetic 125mph speedometer replaces Chronometric.

1965
Fork stanchions 1in longer, lighter external springs. Revised handlebar, thicker tank knee-grips.

1966
New steering head with 62-degree steering angle replacing 65-degree, bottom yoke revision increases steering lock. Slimmer fuel tank with new badges, parcel rack disappears on US models. Full-width hub at front and new brake drum at rear.

Engine number is stamped below cylinder base flange on drive side. Numbers were stamped by hand, so depth and alignment are often less than perfect.

1967
Lucas encapsulated alternator stator. Smiths 150mph speedometer replaces 125mph type. Seat top quilted but still with grey top, black sides, white piping and grey lower trim. Last year of US TT Special.

1968
Amal Concentric carburettors. Independently adjustable contact breakers in deeper timing cover. Twelve-point cylinder base nuts. More heavily braced swinging arm and shuttle valve damping in front fork. Twin-leading-shoe front brake. Air filters standard. Thicker seat padding on hinged base finished in either two-tone or black.

1969
Revised front brake operation and cable run. Parcel rack disappears. Heavier crankshaft flywheel and Nitrided camshafts. Engine number stamped over Triumph logos on raised pad. New fuel tank with thinner knee-grips and simpler badges. Fork yokes altered for wider-section front tyre. Revised seat with passenger grab rail. Balanced exhaust system.

1970
Adjustable pre-load on rear shock absorbers. Grab rail mounted on rear sub-frame. Large Windtone horns, lower seat.

1971
First year of oil-bearing duplex frame. Oil tank replaced by side panel, mirrored on the opposite side. New forks with internal springs, hard-chromed stanchions and bare alloy sliders with four-bolt wheel spindle caps. Headlamp mounted on chromed wire bracket. Squared-off tank for UK models, along with new stands, chainguard, engine plates, mudguards and megaphone-type silencers. Conical hubs front and rear, twin-leading-shoe front brake with integral air scoop. New seat finished in black with quilted and dimpled cover. Rubber-mounted new-type speedometer and tachometer. Direction indicators standard.

1972
Five-speed model (T120V) introduced alongside four-speeder. Frame lowered at rear and seat thinned to reduce height. New cylinder head with push-in exhaust fitting. Extra central stay on front mudguard.

1973
T140 model launched. Initially 724cc, later 744cc, with ten-bolt cylinder head, five-speed gearbox. T140 has revised side panels and ignition switch moved from left side panel to left fork shroud. Revised forks to accommodate 10in disc front brake. Mudguards chrome-plated.

1974
Quieter silencers with reversed-taper end section. Production ceased due to industrial action shortly after the start of 1974 model production in October 1973.

1975
Residual stocks of machines released to dealers. Essentially these were as 1974 models. T120 650cc model dropped.

1976
Left-foot change and hydraulic rear disc brake introduced. Changes to primary drive cover and rear section of frame necessary to facilitate this change.

1977
Limited Jubilee Bonneville with extra chrome, and red, blue and silver paint scheme.

1978
Chromed upper fork shrouds, Veglia instruments on some machines. T140E model launched with revised engine breathing. Chromed mudguards on US exports.

1979
Amal Mark II carburettors standard, cylinder head revised to suit. T140D Special with Lester wheels, stepped seat, black and gold finish. Knee-grips dropped. Hubs polished and lacquered, chromed mudguards standard. Negative-earth electrics adopted with three-phase charging system.

1980
T140ES with electric start launched in April. Starter motor requires modified timing cover. Rear brake caliper mounted above swinging arm on all machines, as on previous year's T140D models. Veglia instruments on all models.

1981
Push-over exhausts re-introduced. Stainless steel mudguards across the range. Executive with twin front discs, fairing and matching luggage. Also fitted with Morris cast alloy wheels, now standard on T140D Special.

1982
All models could be ordered with twin front discs. New fuel tank with flip-up filler cap. Square-type indicators with black plastic body. All US models plus Executive have Bing CV carburettors and Marzocchi rear suspension units.

1983
Custom-style TSX model with cosmetic stickers, 16in rear wheel, short silencers, painted mudguards, low seat, high handlebars. TSS with eight-valve cylinder head. Both models plus UK T140E have alloy Morris wheels. Spoked wheels standard for US. No fork gaiters.

COLOUR SCHEMES

Model year	UK	USA
1959	Pearl Grey and Tangerine	Pearl Grey and Tangerine
	Pearl Grey and Azure Blue	–
1960	Pearl Grey and Azure Blue	Pearl Grey and Azure Blue
1961	Sky Blue and Silver Sheen	Sky Blue and Silver Sheen
1962	Flame and Silver Sheen	Flame and Silver Sheen
1963	Alaskan White	Alaskan White
1964	Gold and Alaskan White	Gold and Alaskan White
1965	Pacific Blue and Silver	Pacific Blue and Silver
1966	Grenadier Red and Alaskan White	Alaskan White, Grenadier Red stripes
1967	Aubergine and Alaskan White	Aubergine and Gold
	–	Aubergine and Alaskan White
1968	Hi Fi Scarlet and Silver	Hi Fi Scarlet and Silver
1969	Olympic Flame and Silver	Olympic Flame and Silver
1970	Astral Red and Silver	Astral Red and Silver
1971	Tiger Gold and Black	Tiger Gold and Black
1972	Tiger Gold and Cold White	Tiger Gold and Cold White
1973	Hi Fi Vermillion and Gold	Hi Fi Vermillion and Gold
	Tiger Gold and Cold White (T120)	–
1974	Cherokee Red and Cold White	Cherokee Red and Cold White
	Purple and Cold White (T120)	Purple and Cold White (T120)
1975	Cherokee Red and Cold White	Cherokee Red and Cold White
	Purple and Cold White (T120)	Purple and Cold White (T120)
1976	Polychromatic Red and Cold White	Polychromatic Red and Cold White
	Polychromatic Blue and Cold White	–
1977	Polychromatic Blue and Cold White	Polychromatic Red and Cold White
		Polychromatic Blue and Cold White
	Silver and Blue (T140J)	Silver and Blue (T140J)
1978	Tawny Brown and Gold	Tawny Brown and Gold
	Aquamarine and Silver	Astral Blue and Silver
	–	Black and Crimson
1979	Black and Red	Dark Blue and Silver
	Beige and Gold	Black and Silver
	–	Candy Apple Red and Black
	Black, gold lines (T140D)	Black, gold lines (T140D)
1980	Steel Grey and Candy Apple Red	Black and Candy Apple Red
	Black , white lines	Olympic Flame and Black
	–	Steel Grey and Black
	Black, gold lines (T140D)	Black, gold lines (T140D)
1981	Black and Candy Apple Red	Smoked Astral Blue and Silver
	Steel Grey and Candy Apple Red	Smoked Olympic Flame and Gold
	Silver Blue and Black	–
	Black, gold lines	–
	Smokey Blue, gold lines	–
	Smokey Flame, gold lines	–
1982	Black, gold lines	Smokey Flame and Ivory
	Smokey Flame and Gold	Smokey Blue and Silver
	Smokey Blue and Gold	Silver Blue and Black
	–	Black and Candy Apple Red
	Smokey Flame, gold lines (Executive)	Smokey Flame, gold lines (Executive)
	Black, gold lines (Executive)	–
	Chrome and Black (Royal, standard)	Black, gold stripes (Royal, standard)
	Chrome and Silver Blue (Royal, deluxe)	–
1983	Black and Candy Apple Red	Black and Candy Apple Red
	Burgundy, gold lines	Burgundy, gold lines
	Black, gold lines	Black, gold lines
	Black, red/orange/yellow stripes (TSX)	Black, red/orange/yellow stripes (TSX)
	Burgundy, red/orange/yellow stripes (TSX)	Gypsy Red, red/orange/yellow stripes (TSX)
	Black, gold lines (TSS)	Black, gold lines (TSS)
	Smokey Red (Executive)	Smokey Red (Executive)
	Smokey Blue (Executive)	Smokey Blue (Executive)

Note From 1979, all specifications and finishes were available to order in all markets.

Frame number stamping on left of front downtube, seen on a US-market 1970 T120R.

Index